LEFT TURN ONLY

Dispatches From The Progressive Underground

LEFT TURN ONLY

Dispatches From The Progressive Underground

2003 - 2009

Written by
BRAD PARKER

Edited with
MARGIE MURRAY

With co-writing contributions from:

Ahjamu Makalani
(A Progressive Plan)
Ahjamu Makalani, Wayne Williams
(Leading Our Way)
Mark Pash
(Progressive Economic Principles)

ISBN - 978-0-578-03846-9
Library of Congress Control Number: 2009910112

Cover design:
Leavy Design Group

Back cover photo:
Wayne Williams

Published by Riozen Media
First printed in Fall 2009 with Book Surge

Riozen Media
PO BOX 261931
Encino CA
91426-1931
Email: riozen@riozen.com
Website: www.riozen.com

to my wife,

IDA ROSE

the truest soul of all,
who makes the dream possible

Left Turn Only

Acknowledgements

First and foremost, I am completely indebted to my mother, Johanna Rashid Parker Klibanoff, for my sense of civic duty and political purpose. Since my first foray into politics in high school, she has never wavered in her belief in my possibilities, my policies or me. She leads by example, with her community activism that continues to inspire me, when I attempt to do the impossible. My brothers, Scott, Bill and David, have been the rigorous sounding post and rancorous debate society that every policy theorist needs to prepare for the fire of dissent. Even my father, Robert N. Parker, a staunch conservative Republican, has helped to sharpen my wits. Through this entire whirligig of political turmoil, my stepfather Mordecai Klibanoff and my stepmother Patricia McCambridge have balanced the equation with understanding and support. Then, there are my children, Saida and Abraham, my stepchildren, April and Eric, my son-in-law Eric, and my grandchildren, Hannah and Otto, who are the very reason I invest a large part of my private life to the public good. They embody the essence of my motto - further.

I am an energized member of the Progressive Swarm, without whose support, guidance and collaboration the opportunity to have my voice heard would not be possible. I want to thank the many Progs, who I owe the deepest gratitude to, with a deep bow.

Most of all, I tip my hat to my editor - Margie Murray. Her guidance in the compiling of Left Turn Only and inspiration to share my political essays makes this book her work as much as mine.

Next, are my closest allies who have organized, strategized and co-written with me over these years: Johanna Olson, Ahjamu Makalani and Wayne Williams. We have spent many late nights and early mornings planning the "impossible."

To Lila Garrett, I am forever in her debt. She schooled me in the art of "on the air" progressive radio. Lila always cuts to the true heart of the matter and tells it like it is. When she lays it down - we pick it up.

My other co-writer, featured in LTO, is Mark Pash, who drew out for me the big financial picture, regarding Progressive Economics. Of course, there are my fellow VDU writers-in-arms: Jerry Drucker and Robert Illes, who witicized my diatribes. To the all of the progressive writers I have had the honor to be included with in many online publications - Valley Democrats United Newsletter, MB Civic, LA Progressive, The Huffington Post, Daily Kos, No Quarter - write on!

Many bows and boundless kudos to Cathy Leavy for the inspired cover and Wayne Williams for making me look good in the photo.

These Progressive activists have helped me to keep it real and livened up the proceedings wherever we have gone: Mimi Kennedy, Tim Carpenter, Marcy Winograd, Teddi Winograd, Ted

Williams, Marsha Williams, Tom Hayden, Joye Swan, Mary Pallant, Leah Herzberg, Liz Knipe, Annette St. John Lawrence, Wendy Block, Sam Park, Julie Sanford, Jon Williams, Dr. Bill Honigman, Cindy Asner, Jeffrey Killeen, Linda Sutton, Christine Pelosi, Lee Frank, Laura Bonham, Dick and Sharon Price, John and Patty Garamendi, Chip Forrester, Mervis Reissig, Erin Flynn, Judy Alter, Ricco Ross, Dorothy Reik, Julie Lopez-Dad, Norman Solomon, Steve Fine, Mark and Ruth Hull-Richter, Stan West, Harlan Hobgood, Maureen Cruise, Susan Haskell, Cara Robin, Ferial Masry, Michael Butler, Richard Greene, Paul Berenson, Paul Koretz, Linda Milazzo, Dolores Press, Ann Hiller, Ellen Brucke, Chris Murray, Zack Webber, Susan Lerner, Paula Berinstein, Mary Sue Maurer, Illene Proctor, Ralph Ericsson, Monique Pernell, David Dayen, Tom Camarella, John and Elizabeth Edwards, Bobbie and Placido Salazar, Dante Atkins, Dana Dean, Kevin Lynn, Cynthia Matthews, Robert Silver, Lillian Laskin, Gay Lannon, Barbara Levin, Dan Licht, Renee Lancon, Flo Webber, Jill Barad, Mary Jacobs, Diane Shamis, Alice Lynn, Julia Brownley, Carole Luteness, Michelle Hutchins, Elizabeth Badger, Barry Groveman, Medea Bengeman, Jodie Evans, Cathlyn Daly, Paul Burke, Tim Goodrich, Bob Handy, Gar Byrum, Miguel Santiago, Len Chaitin, Chris Robson, Charles Coleman, William Crain, Ferris Gluck, Shirley Hunley, Lawrence Lebo, Kate Wallace, Peter and Marcy Rothenberg, Erin Prangley, Elke Heitmeyer, Fran Pavley, John Heaner, Dan Tamm, Brian Leubitz, Eric Bauman, Tom O'Shaughnessy and so many others.

Lastly, I should thank the clubs and organizations that I have been a member and officer of these crucial years: Valley Democrats United, Progressive Democrats of Los Angeles, the Progressive Caucus of the California Democratic Party, Progressive Democrats of America and the California Democratic Party.

I want to make a special deep bow to Tim Carpenter and Mimi Kennedy who formed and have guided Progressive Democrats of America through these turbulent years. They are the only truly Progressive national organization I know of. PDA knows what it stands for - the unvarnished truth and the way forward. It has been my pleasure to be an early member of PDA and to help found several of its chapters including PDLA.

Being part of the "Progressive Swarm," as it formed and informed, has been the highest honor. It has instilled in me the spirit of our ancestors who taught us to always; Stand Up, Show Up and Speak Up because, Now is the Time, This is the Place and We are the People.

Brad Parker
Los Angeles, CA
September 2009

Left Turn Only

Dedication

Acknowledgements

Table of Contents

Prelude

Part I - Past, Present and Future

Part II - Futuring the California Democratic Party

Part III - Stand Up, Show Up & Speak Up

Part IV - Progressive Voice

Part V - America Redux

Part VI - Dems in D'Town

Part VII - Progressive Economics

CODA

Left Turn Only

Prelude

Primping electeds memorizing their dumbed-down diatribe for the bloviating bobble heads of the mass infotainment matrix. Bundling lobbyists scuffling off to the five star country club soirees where they'll pick the pockets of the showboats of industrial retrograde. Just another day in the paradise of the binging crony pigs snorting as they gobble up the hard-earned truffles of public taxes, whilst they float merrily down the Potomac.

Yes, dear reader, this is America in the 21st century. No, not your America or my America but the America of the super-rich, the ultra-rich and the I'll bet the ranch rich. They own it all and - because they have corrupted the emaciated corpses of both of the political parties, which allowed them to seize the rusty wheel of the ship of state - they control it all as well. It was into this mise en scene strode, like Kurosawa's Seven Samurai, the Progressives.

Past is Prologue. In his seminal vivisection of the Crown and the Church - *Dictionnaire philosophique* - Voltaire rallied the minds and hearts of the "Enlightenment" in everlasting vigilance against the "privileged orthodoxy" of the ruling elite. He sent the inquiring spirit off in search of the "true and the good." He wryly pointed humanity toward the "day of reason." Along with Jefferson, Franklin, Hamilton, Kant, Hume, Locke, Gouges, Pombal, Montesquieu, Paine, Tocqueville,

Spinoza, Wollstonecraft and nameless others, the evolutionary idea of government of, by and for the people was imagined and then brought to brilliant fruition in the American Revolution. That very struggle for freedom and independence is alive in the Progressive Movement today.

We came to be known as the Progressives after abandoning the more static label, Liberals - that had received such a fraudulent beating at the hands of the officious right wing pundits and apologist moderates in the Mass Media cyclotron of Babel. Over time, we began to realize common threads in our aspirations and analysis. These commonalities have coalesced into a movement - citizens collaborating on modern processes and cogent policy for political change - the Progressive Movement - or, as I prefer - the Progressive Swarm. In the last five years, we have spawned the ongoing eruptions of political courage from the left side of the spectrum and challenged the neo-cons public chicanery and private avarice. We are squarely in the face of the status quotarians.

Aggressive Progressives - that's what they call us.

Many of us, who are veterans of the political movements of the Sixties and Seventies, recognized, after the election of 2000, that resistance to Crony politics, government and business would not be possible through the old school street demonstrations alone. We, grizzled agitators of the evanescent past, knew the limits and lessons of the streets and the suites. We needed a more immediate way to communicate and organize with each other. Then, out of the blue, emerged the paradigm shift that brought us the possibilities that could level the playing field - the Internet or more importantly, our appreciation and use of it. Its birth, however, was a long time comin'.

Eventually, we realized that with the ubiquitous always-on person-to-person connectivity of the World Wide Web, an infrastructure of organizing and activism could be developed that might remove the deficit of citizen involvement in Democratic Party and American policy-making (lack of a lasting political infrastructure was the unfinished business of the preceding Liberal movements). By providing the democratization of information, the Internet was hooking up the bottom without the top knowing what was happening thereby creating a seismic shift in political organizing - especially in the Democratic Party.

Together - inside and outside the political system - Progressives began to operate as a "swarm" - as defined by the "swarm intelligence" models of science. That is, Progressives are more self-actuated and less in need of leaders to tell them what to do next. Citizens are stepping up, standing up, showing up and speaking up all across America without any woman or man on a white horse leading the charge. The members are the leaders.

Defenders of the status quo fear the swarm. Their fear is based on the idea that only they, the controllers, can manage the affairs of state and guide us to a better tomorrow. However, in a stunning twist of fate -

Control has failed. In our new paradigm, of the upside down pyramid - Facilitation is the key to the future.

Crony corporate interests and the ultra-rich global players who control the planet's wealth stole the government, business and politics out from under us, while we were derelict in our vigilance and too self-absorbed to care. After decades of gorging on the productivity of the working class, they are no longer capable of operating any of these systems effectively. In their stupefied smugness, Crony corporate bureaucracies, political parties and governments, hobbled by incumbency, endorsements, big money donors and top-down tyrannies, are not able to adapt to our new paradigm of interconnectedness, as evidenced by their spectacular loss of competency in all current economic and social crises.

Progressives sensed this intuitively and now, by communicating with each other across the Internet, we have shared the evidence of this stupendous theft. Our government and business leaders have failed us and even their gagged and bound mass media have been unable to disguise the extent of their malfeasance. Like the survivors of hurricane Katrina - we know that the only people we can rely on to change society are each other. We are on our own.

Is there any hope? Yes, but not from politicians. We, with our inertia and our fear, are the cause of this calamity. Therefore, we must become the cure. Horizontal and universal communications, streaming through the light fibers and wireless crossroads of the Internet, unimpeded by profit interests, will yield an educated public, making the bold positive choices necessary to grapple with the dislocation of globalized realities. Only a responsible citizenry, allied with facilitating governments and economies, is capable of creating a new vision of governance and commerce. The Progressive Movement is the first political sign of this rising consciousness and paradigm shift.

All of the essays, articles and actions included in this book were originally published and disseminated in the micro media.

Not unlike the pamphleteering of the American Revolutionary era, micro media - peer-to-peer Internet communication - has come to rival and engulf mass media. Micro media consists of the following elements of facilitation: email, enewsletters, eaction alerts, eorganizing, blogging, websites, list-serves, egroups (Yahoo, Google etc.) social networks and more innovations, like microblogging, coming online everyday. Our transformative media is beyond the grasp of Crony filters and myopic Madison Avenue focus groups. It is the power of user-generated content. It is the long tail of creativity. It is the liberating democratization of information. Coursing along micro media's digitized river of electrons we have discovered each other, our potential and the future.

And so it began - the Progressive Movement. Without even a casual contemplation of its imaginable impact or the architecture of its sibilating electronic veins, we set sail on the quixotic simplicity of the micro media to lands unknown. Slowly, unnoticeably, an abstruse surge of truth began to swamp the obfuscation of the ruling elite. The Progressive Swarm was forming and informing, first outside the political mainstream and then headlong into the Democratic Party Apparatus.

In 2005, without much fanfare, awareness of our path and of each other coalesced across the country into an unanticipated amalgamation of activists from divergent backgrounds entering into "inside the Party" politics within the various state Democratic Parties. Here in California, it centered on the formation of a "Progressive Caucus" inside the California Democratic Party. Ours is the largest state Democratic Party in the nation and it has proven to be the ideal place to confront the "privileged orthodoxy of the ruling elite." What we did not realize in 2005, when the Progressive Caucus was formed, was the extent to which the entrails of the Democratic Party machine were corrupted.

As Tom Hayden once remarked, these were "good people caught up in a bad system." However, they were all too happy to blame the system rather than change it. We were not so inclined.

For my part, as a card-carrying member of the Progressive Swarm, I have focused on utilizing the micro media to organize our movement inside the Democratic Party and promote our platform. The planks of this platform include: an end to the occupation of Iraq and the dismantling of the American military-industrial complex, bringing to justice all of the violators of the public trust of the last several years - either Republican, Democrat or Independent, establishing secure, voter owned and verifiable voting systems, full public campaign financing - Clean Money, progressive economic policy that will contend with the causes of poverty and pollution while promoting the local, sustainable, renewable and humane underpinnings of a new global people-before-profit business framework. Of course, there are many more essential planks but this would be an unrivaled change of course and an admirable beginning. Progressives are ambitious and determined and this book is a chronicle of our journey in California from 2003 to 2009 by an observer and participant.

It was at the California Democratic Party convention in 2005 that the first in the nation resolution calling for an end to the War in Iraq was passed. I had the honor that day of giving the speech in favor of the resolution to the assembled body of more than two thousand delegates. Our victory was difficult to achieve, with the PLEOs (party leaders and elected officials) scurrying about backstage furiously devising parliamentary procedures to squelch the will of the people but we prevailed. Those same characters have been bedeviled by us ever since.

In the spirit and reality of "swarm intelligence theory", the Progressive movement has acted not so much with leaders as with the leadership of the members. The members know the issues and decide the actions to take. So, we dubbed ourselves - the Progressive Swarm. I am sure that to the leadership of the Democratic Party, Republicans and the Crony captains of business, we seem like an angry swarm ready to sting. Not so.

We are making the sweet honey of justice, equality and truth to feed the minds of the public, inspire them to demand the best from their government, stand up, show up and speak up. As Petey Green would say, "we're just keepin' it real."

We have divided the collected works into six parts. The first part contains my three main theses that have been recurrent themes throughout the writings of these last five years: the Republicans, the DLC and the Progressive movement blueprint. Part Two is more or less a chronology of the Progressive advent in the California Democratic Party. Part Three is a group of principled stands I have taken over the years. Part Four is some radio commentaries I have made on the Progressive movement. Part Five is a series of commentaries on the American body politic. I conclude with Part Six on Progressive economics. Progressive social policy has become the political dialogue and debate of the nation. I believe that economics and a Progressive point of view on economics will become the leading policy discussion in the coming years.

America is entering a hopeful era of political life with Democrats in the majority in Congress and President Barack H. Obama in the White House. Much will be expected of this shift in power. Much will be demanded. Our troubles, inherited from the last thirty years of lack luster and fraudulent political delinquency, will not easily be remedied.

As much as I wish good fortune to the new federal leadership, I call for renewed vigilance from the citizens of this Republic.

As this book goes to print President Obama and the Democratic Congress are being hammered on the anvil of "Stand and Deliver." At this point, in the fall of 2009, it is not possible to make a clear prediction on whether the latest Democratic incarnation in D.C. will be up to the test of the times – the epic struggle with CRONY corporate power and its death grip on the American government at every level. On the vital issues of War, Healthcare, Environment, Economics etc. the jury is out. The outcome of this battle for the soul of the Democratic Party and America will be the subject of future books. Stay tuned and stay vigilant.

These dispatches were underground - in the micro media - until now. (We have kept them in their original form as much as possible. The format for the articles is in "blog" form rather than standard book form to preserve their historical context. Left Turn Only is an anthology of history and analysis as well as a how-to manual of the Progressive Movement). They chronicle the beginning of the first great political movement of the 21st century at the western edge of the American experiment. I hope you derive some benefit and understanding from this compendium of essays, articles and actions of the Progressive Movement in California. I offer them to you and yours as an inspiration from a few brave souls who are changing the world. May they motivate you to act and act Progressively. After so many hard right turns politically over the last four decades, America can only be revived with a solid left turn - a

Progressive left turn. It may be a slow turn or unforeseen cataclysmic events may propel it at a greater pace but I believe it will be in the end a - *Left Turn Only.*

Only by investing part of our private life in the public good can we realize what so many have striven to create in this American dream, the realization of the Liberal Ideal. For our ancestors, our descendants and ourselves, let us pledge to each other our commitment to the diligent principled evolution of democracy.

Now is the Time. This is the Place. We are the People.

further...

Brad Parker

Left Turn Only *~ Dispatches From The Progressive Underground ~ by a participant and observer...*

Part I

Past, Present & Future

the REPUBLICAN ANARCHY COLLECTIVE
(or the end of civilization as we need it)

October 2005

Now is the soporific summer of the Republican's Ronald Reagan-Howard Jarvis disconnect made acrid winter by the son of Bush, the bumbling buffoon from Crawford, land of the kooky Texas millionaires - as Eisenhower so affectionately referred to them. The year was 2004 and the culmination of decades of prefabrication, plotting and deception had at last born fruit. Republicans were obstinately in control of all branches of the federal government. "Make way for the Conservative millennium" they chortled.

From the first days of their arrival, in 1994, bandying the bogus "contract" about the capitol steps, there was something about this particular confederation of extreme right-wingers that seemed queasily malevolent; something that didn't smack of politics as usual. Now it's 2005 and their once great expectations, pummeled by recent setbacks have given way to reveal some of the backroom operations behind this gang of provocateurs. Even so, many questions remain to be answered. Why would they want to become the government when their enmity for it drives them to, as they have said, "drown it in a bathtub"? What ominous rumination has been smuggled into Washington DC inside of their baggage? Who are these people?

For the answers we must look beneath the thin veneer of equivocation proffered by the Republican spin machine, beyond the mocking tirades of the talk jocks. As we examine this cabal, remind yourself that not all political partisans are operating under the same rules or after the same ends. For radicals like this bunch, the opposite of logic and rational thought, or rules, is more suited to their purposes, especially when their inherited delusions seem to them to be the rules. Anything goes for this crowd.

This iteration of the Republican Party should rightly be known as the "Republican Anarchy Collective." How it transformed itself, and to what ends, is a complex story. But before an explanation of the RAC and its motives is offered, two definitions should be considered to guide our examination:

Anarchy
Noun: A state of lawlessness and disorder (usually resulting from a failure of government) [syn: lawlessness] - Absence of any form of political authority - Political disorder and confusion.

Civilization
Noun: An advanced state of intellectual, cultural, and material development in human society, marked by progress in the arts and sciences, the extensive use of record-keeping, including writing, and the appearance of complex political and social institutions.

Source ~ Dictionary.com Unabridged (v 1.1) Based on the Random House Unabridged Dictionary, © Random House, Inc. 2006.

Armed with only these two simple definitions, we can begin to see where the Republican Anarchy Collective is taking America: a very Roman brand of "anarchy" and an end to "civilization" as we need it. Hence, whereas to the Democratic, Liberal and Progressive majority of citizens the RAC seems to be unhinged from principle, they are in fact following a precisely laid out plan formed over 70 years: a plan to dismantle the government, except for the military and behavior police, civilization for the few and anarchy for the many.

The New Deal

Franklin Delano Roosevelt was a politician with bold transformative ideas. Even though he was a member of the privileged coterie, he consciously fractured their traditions, when he set out to establish a more perfect union. His generation of Democrats changed the very purpose of government in America. The New Deal ushered in "civilization" for the broad working class. Franklin took the progressive achievements of his cousin Theodore to new heights with the Social Security Act, the Fair Labor Standards Act, the National Labor Relations Act, the Federal Deposit Insurance Corporation, the Public Works Administration, the National Recovery Act, the Securities Act of 1933, the Federal Emergency Relief Administration and so many more audacious legislative initiatives.

As momentous as these programs proved to be for the majority of Americans, used to being drowned in the changing seas of economic turmoil, they were not cherished by many of the sons and daughters of industrial wealth. As soon as they became law, a long-term plan was set in motion to turn back the clock to the anarchy of the "Gilded Age of the Robber Barons." Wealthy patrons of the Republican Party were determined to regain control of the destiny of the nation and put the riff-raff back where they belonged, in the gutter.

The Wilderness

From 1932 through 1964, the Conservative Republicans suffered under the emergence of the middle class. Thrashing about against the dangers of sin and lefties among us, they alternately created momentary lapses of national ethics and lasting injustices, aimed at the citizens they despised - anyone without lots of money or of a different ethnicity. In the Sixties and Seventies, no longer just a bunch of rich kooks from Texas, they forged a new alliance, a collective, with the radical religious and sociopathic right.

Ultra right-wing activists, like Robert Welch and Phyllis Schlafly as well as John Stormer from the John Birch Society, became principal players in the Goldwater Presidential campaign of 1964, carrying with them the "new conservative" torch. They, among others, provided the delusional paranoia of all things "liberal" that was tempered into the Republican Party platform. William F. Buckley Jr. put an intellectual patina on the corrosive creed that was veering away from mere "no taxes" to "no government" (except for the beau monde). Liberal Republicans, like Nelson Rockefeller, Lowell Weicker, John Lindsay and Earl Warren, were no longer welcome in the Grand Old Party of Abraham Lincoln (are there any true Republicans of Lincoln left?). To the waggish glee of the RAC, the emergence of the counter-culture in the Sixties pushed the Republicans further out of the mainstream. With the flourishing of the counter culture, and the animus coming from the far right to it, the seeds were sown for a paradigm shift within the Republican Party.

Thick face, Black heart
(Neo-Cons and the ghosts of Stalin, Mao, and Trotsky)

During the Seventies, the trifecta of the conservative Republican industrialists, religious fanatics and sociopathic underdogs fused into what we now know as the Republican Anarchy Collective. Each had their particular need and each thought it was getting the best end of the bargain. Industrialists wanted a roll back of the New Deal and a wide-open unregulated market. Fundamentalists wanted a Christian nation based on their spectacularly intolerant and medieval version of what they claim the Bible says. Sociopaths wanted, well, any outcome that would exact revenge upon all of the citizens they reviled. Down at the crossroads, their deal with the devil was struck and all they needed was a plan. In the newly dubbed "neo-con" movement, they all found what they were looking for.

The RAC wanted to dismantle the government, except for the military. Neo-cons led by Grover Norquist, Paul Wolfowitz, Natan Sharansky, Richard Perle, Lewis "Scooter" Libby, Irving Kristol, Norman Podhoretz, Jeanne Kirkpatrick, William Kristol, John Podhoretz, Max Boot, William Bennet, Dick Cheney, Donald Rumsfeld, Robert Novak, Jerry Falwell, Pat Robertson, James Dobson, Ralph Reed, Paul Weyrich, Tim LaHaye and others provided them with the ideological impetus to get the job done. These chattering-class officious and pseudo-religious grifters also provided an over-arching strategy, which they had perversely found the basis for in the ashes of Communism.

Deriving specious intellectual legitimacy from the writings of Max Shachtman, Leo Strauss and James Burnham, many Neo-cons had drifted from the hard left of the Marxist-Leninist politics of their youth to the hard right of Goldwater and Reagan. Like other neo-cons, Jeanne Kirkpatrick was far to the left and a member of the Youth section of the American Socialist Party in the Sixties. She, along with Paul Wolfowitz and Richard Perle, was a member of, "Social Democrats USA" in the early Seventies. They were all followers of ex-Trotskyite Max Shachtman. Along with Shachtman, they decried the inevitable results of the Bolshevik revolutions. Socialism and communism had failed to live up to their utopian vision.

However, even though they had become disillusioned by the harsh reality of the Soviet

Union of Stalin and Communist China of Mao, their disdain did not disavow them of their concrete belief in control of the state by a strong central government under the control of one leader (the old Hobbesian Emperor with new clothes). In fact, they were convinced that "orthodoxy" must be strictly enforced in political thought and that "free-thinking" was anathema to the cohesion of the state. Dissent was to them the greatest liability of the "liberal ideal" and encouraged moral weakness.

In their febrile reasoning, top-down Stalinist-style state control would combine with the military to achieve new global objectives. Corporations would become the state. Markets would be opened and maintained by the military masking itself as Democracy Liberator. "Free Enterprise" would be their new mantra of political progress. The political objectives changed but the strategy remained the same. Hence, aggressive corporatism and oligarchic democracy, given birth by conflict, were to be the new hegemony. With riotous evangelical fervor, the RAC set out to lead the new "perpetual revolution." Old left had become new right.

Paradox or Paradise?

Alexander Hamilton's eloquent arguments in favor of a durable government include this cautionary passage from the Federalist Papers No. 1, "On the other hand, it will be equally forgotten that the vigor of government is essential to the security of liberty; that, in the contemplation of a sound and well-informed judgment, their interest can never be separated; and that a dangerous ambition more often lurks behind the specious mask of zeal for the rights of the people than under the forbidden appearance of zeal for the firmness and efficiency of government. History will teach us that the former has been found a much more certain road to the introduction of despotism than the latter, and that of those men who have overturned the liberties of republicans, the greatest number have begun their career by paying an obsequious court to the people; commencing demagogues, and ending tyrants."

And so it is with the RAC - as their crusade has taken them from obscurity to near complete control of the federal and most state governments. It all began with Reagan (former Democrat and president of a union) and the Sagebrush Rebellion, promising to return the government to the people, end over-taxation and democratize the world. Using the specter of the Soviet boogeyman, they pumped the public with a delirious fear of the impending nuclear apocalypse. The agitated crowd ate it up and slowly voted RAC acolytes into office, at every level of government. Timorous Democrats, goaded by Elaine Kamarck and William Galston's apologist broadside, "The Politics of Evasion", capitulated to the swaggering RAC by ditching the "Liberal" wing of the party and forming the Democratic Leadership Council, funded by corporations, promising to make America safe for business again and ending welfare as we know it.

All Democrats got was; two terms for Clinton/Gore (they both exited to wealthy upwardly mobile lifestyles) and the loss of every branch of government on the federal level and most of the states as well. However, the DLC, having fallen into the trap baited by their own weakness (i.e. stand for nothing, don't offend anyone, lunge to the middle) did affirm the RAC theory of, "business knows best" and firmly placed corporations on the new alter of governance. The stage was now set for the final ascendancy of the RAC. Financed and directed by their main political action committee - the Council for National Policy - and tenaciously in control of the government, they could now dismantle it without restraint. Having bought up, FOX-bludgeoned and castrated the major media, there would be no voice of dissent or reporter reporting it.

As Hamilton had predicted, they promised reform and delivered it with a vengeance. However, every machine needs some mechanics and tools to keep it running and the RAC is no exception. To keep their contraption in action, they've called on some of the darkest minds in the history of politics.

Tool Kit

How the RAC took over the government is first the result of tactics formulated and operated by Lee Atwater, Richard Viguerie, Roger Ailes, Frank Luntz, Grover Norquist, Karl Rove and their minions. These RAC consultants came together and over the last thirty years, and with numerous dirty-trick campaigns, succeeded where other misanthropes had failed. Through the clever and deceptive use of language, direct mail and TV ads, they played upon the public's weaknesses, principally intolerance, racism, fear and greed, and delivered victory after victory to the RAC. Code words like "Sanctity of Marriage," "Secular Humanism," "No Quotas," "Faith Based," "Fair and Balanced," "Liberal Elites", Compassionate Conservative", "School Vouchers" and "Culture of Life," masked the true identity of the anti-civil rights, racist and intolerant initiatives they represented. California's infamous "Prop. 13" promise of "Lower Taxes" was the front for "No Taxes." With no taxes collected, social programs could be effectively eradicated along with public education and environmental protection. Budget deficits, exacerbated by tax cuts, are key to drying up the money available for social programs. "Starve the Beast" (i.e. the government) is right next to "in God We Trust" in the RAC lexicon.

Secondly, the RAC perpetual revolution is funded in a surreptitious and novel way by the "War on Drugs." This heinous military police action is a pet project of the RAC and various beguiled Democrats. Illegal drugs and the money derived from their unregulated and untaxed sale is the mother of all slush funds. Nations, police departments, politicians, judges, gangs and terrorists are in on the take. A lunatic game of cops and robbers has destabilized the entire world.

To the RAC this is manna from heaven. Only in an apparent state of anarchy could the government institute and maintain draconian laws invading personal property, privacy rights and political organizing. Plus, who knows how much of the ocean of black market money goes to RAC purposes like it did in the Iran-Contra scandal? We do know that it is the main source of funding for terrorists. Without radicals of every stripe blowing up the globe, would a military-police action on every corner be acceptable? The so-called "War on Drugs" funds the swamp that breeds the terrorists, whose eradication funds the military police, a perfect hideous symmetry. Also, would the land of the free and the home of the brave have the highest per capita ratio of citizens in prison in the world without illegal drugs? Drug related offenders take up half of the room in American prisons, conveniently keeping hordes of young agitators off the streets and providing expansive pools of diverted public cash for contributions to RAC coffers from the prison guard's unions and prison operators.

Finally, there is the clamor of "governmental religious intolerance." How deft the RAC has been at decrying the absence of God in the deliberations of the State. Putting the government into our bedrooms and out of our boardrooms, as well putting God back into the courtrooms, has been the penultimate success of the RAC. Personal behavior has been demonized to better effectuate the frenzy of the new law and order. Bollixed believers have eagerly voted against themselves in the name of faith and piety. Meanwhile, the men and women behind the curtain giggle as they dispatch John Bolton to the U.N., not to burn it down but to blithely neuter it by promulgating the mold of obfuscation and vexation. Outside, the masses are swarming in anger.

Why has the RAC gone to such extremes to trash the American liberal Ideal? Because, the mob, having been given torches and provocation, merrily marches to the castle and burns it down. Remember what Ronnie said, "government is not the solution to our problem, government is the problem!"

The New Anarchy

Anarchy from the right is not merely the left's knee-jerk nihilistic model of no government or personal property anarchy but a very special collection of control and lack of control that will breed a new population of cowered and impoverished masses, easily manipulated by greed and fear, and drugged by mindless infotainment. Society will be divided into three classes: owners, workers and military police. The only taxes will be on what the workers buy - a consumption tax for the have-nots. Wages will be reduced to as far as inhumanely possible. Education, healthcare, emergency services and all other civic responsibilities including clean water, air and land will be left up to the individual. Just like New Orleans after hurricane Katrina tore through, we will be on our own.

The only services provided will be for the owners or the have-gots. Military police will enforce order domestically and abroad without constraint. Dissent will not be tolerated and will be punished severely. No "right of privacy" will exist. Personal behavior decisions will be made by the state in the name of "public morality." Corporations and the landed aristocracy will not be regulated in any manner. Environmental regulations will be abolished, as the planet will only be seen as a vehicle for wealth creation for the owner caste. Rituals of religious obedience, compliance and observance will be enforced daily upon the worker class. The rights of the owners and their religious advisors will prevail in all cases brought before courts, set up merely to rubber stamp the policies necessary to further the aims of the state. As the last vestiges of the New Deal are given the bum's rush, anything valuable will be "privatized" (pick-pocketed). All American assets held in the "public trust" will be converted to "private interests."

The state will be inherited by succeeding generations of owners, clerics and military police, to their sole benefit (Gaius Julius Caesar would have loved this setup!). Or, perhaps the un-holy trinity of Jewish-Christian-Islamic militants has other plans for the world with their escalating Armageddon in the desert? Nonetheless, nightmares of the Twentieth Century, whether by Orwell, Huxley or Wells, will pale in comparison to the on-coming reality of the Twenty First. If you think this is an exaggeration, then you only have to follow the hellish ooze of legal action flowing from the capitols of the nation to know that this is where the RAC juggernaut, with the aid of so-called moderate Democrats, is furiously careening.

Further?

Like the mythic Charles Foster Kane of Orson Welles famed "Citizen Kane," we might never know the motives of the menacing and delusional

RAC. Perhaps it is as simple as an unhappy childhood, poor self-image or desperation to be listened to. More likely, it is the rich getting richer, playing a dangerous round of roulette with the fate of humanity on the line; life as a casino with the upper crust pulling the strings, hoping no one notices that they are no better at operating the government than King George III and the Church of England were in 1776.

We have come full circle, back to a government of propertied families passing on the seal of state and the fire and brimstone church once again bellowing for its right to judge our very thoughts. It is as if the last three centuries of struggle were for naught. Madison Avenue hucksters, on behalf of the corporate CEO/RAC cartel, dominate the culture. Politics, entertainment, news, religion and sports are now entirely sold as the sizzle not the steak. In fact, there isn't even a steak behind the sizzle at this point. Life has been hollowed out, emptied of resonance, context and warmth and left the vertiginous public listless and fearful. Out of the fear has come blind contempt. Into that void has stepped the RAC. 1984 has finally arrived, only about twenty years late. While we were too busy to be bothered with government, the Republican Anarchy Collective has stolen it with a mixture of guile, deceit, hard work, laziness on our part and brilliant Machiavellian cunning. Now that the mask has been removed from the RAC, we can see who they are and what they are doing. All that remains to be asked is how will we respond?

DLC Democrats and their moderate knaves, who continue to capitulate to the RAC, should take a cue from the old Dixiecrats and join the RAC. They are of no use to the Democrats any longer. Liberals and Progressives who don't rise from the stupor of their endless quest for personal enlightenment and aggrandizement of wealth to participate in the civic life of the nation are equally dysfunctional.

There will be a special place in infamy, not for the RAC but for us, if we let this idea, a free nation, and a beacon to the world, founded upon principles, *"We the People of the United States, in Order to form a more perfect Union, establish Justice, insure domestic Tranquility, provide for the common defence, promote the general Welfare, and secure the Blessings of Liberty to ourselves and our Posterity, do ordain and establish this Constitution for the United States of America" – (Declaration of Independence, 1776) "a government for, by and of the people", (Lincoln's Gettysburg Address, 1863)* perish from the face of the earth because we didn't have the time to engage ourselves in the government of the nation.

If we value civilization and reject anarchy of any kind, we will - wake up. We will organize. We will transform the Democratic Party. We will get Liberal and Progressive candidates elected to every office in the nation, at every level of government and most importantly, hold them accountable. We will stop the RAC madness. It is our sacred duty to all those who came before us and to all those who will come after. In the words of Langston Hughes, "O, let America be America again – The land that never has been yet – And yet must be." We will rise to this serious challenge or die like Mr. Kane with no one left to explain why so much promise was so easily seduced and left to rot in an incandescent pool of self pity and clueless detachment.

Don't be deceived by the current setbacks the RAC is suffering. To the RAC, this is a brawl to the death. Impeachment of Bush or any other loss would only impede their relentless fury not extinguish it. As they say in poker, they're all in. If you ever thought to yourself that you would like to have participated in a watershed moment in the history of humanity, you are in luck. Now is the time. This is the place. We are the People.

The Politics of Capitulation

May 2006

Even a casual perusal of the new magnum dictum of the DLC (Democratic Leadership Council aka The Third Way) reveals the tenuous ties to reality embodied in its extensive pages of charts, statistics, quotes and downright hokum. William A. Galston & Elaine C. Kamarck's latest bromide to the so-called "New Democrats" or moderates, "The Politics of Polarization", is a thinly veiled attempt to salvage any remnant of authenticity that their original broadside, "The Politics of Evasion" claimed to represent and has since lost. If it was only a corporate hack job to keep the nose of the crony capitalist machine poked squarely into the business of DNC deliberations it could be excused with a "politics as usual" sigh of exasperation. However, it is only the latest attempt to disguise the old biases and intolerance in the new clothes of clever strategy and the "win at any cost to our core principles" tactics so thoroughly discredited by the spectacular electoral loss of every branch of the federal government beginning in 1994 to the Republicans.

The DLC and Democratic Party "Hackocracy" incessantly chortle, "Winning at the polls is the only thing that counts in electoral politics!" By their very own yardstick, they are utter failures and need to be dismissed.

I highly recommend that every Liberal and Progressive Democrat read both of Kamarck and

Galston's papers. There is no better way to educate yourself as to whom we are actively opposed by in the upper echelons of the Democratic Party at every level. Let me state for the record what my overall opinion of the DLC, The Third Way, the New Democrats and Kamarck & Galston et al is; they have reduced themselves to being shills for the National Corporate Party that is attempting to control every aspect of American life and they don't even know it. They blithely espouse the latest model of intolerance based on ethnicity, income, gender, age and sexual orientation. "Business is the Business of America," they grimly observe. "Morality is more important than Freedom," they parrot from their perch on the shoulders of the Republican grifters mining the fears of the middle class. If we assume that they are all good people with the best of intentions for the broad working class, and I do, then we must marvel at how far they have drifted from where they started and the alarming negative effect they have had on our party and the nation.

I believe their over-arching self-interests got the best of them along the way and they left the mortals behind as they ascended into the oxygen-deprived atmosphere of the gods in Washington D.C. With Dick Morris as a pioneer of their movement, this comes as no surprise. Now it's time to come back down to earth, back to main street and reaffirm the core values of social justice, equality, opportunity, civil rights, prosperity for all, security through global cooperation, entrepreneurial innovation, environmental enhancement and inclusion that are the hallmarks of Democratic Party's achievements in the

Twentieth Century.

Here are a few pertinent excerpts from "The Politics of Polarization – by William Galston and Elaine Kamarck, 2005". My comments follow each section.

Page 26

Four New Myths That Cloud The Mind And Thwart Change

In "The Politics of Evasion," we wrote of a "systematic denial of reality" that was contributing to the defeat of Democratic candidates for national office. Underpinning this denial were three pervasive "myths" that conveniently excused party leaders, elected incumbents, and activists from critical thinking. "The first [myth] is the belief that Democrats have failed because they have strayed from the true and pure faith of their ancestors — we call this the myth of Liberal Fundamentalism. The second is the belief that Democrats need not alter public perceptions of their party but can regain the presidency by getting current nonparticipants to vote — we call this the Myth of Mobilization. The third is the belief that there is nothing fundamentally wrong with the Democratic Party: there is no realignment going on, and the proof is that Democrats still control the majority of offices below the presidency. We call this the Myth of the Congressional Bastion."

Despite the differences between 1989 and 2005, it is our contention that the Democratic Party is in much the same position as it was in the wake of Michael Dukakis' defeat. As in the late 1980s and early 1990s, the party today is challenged to modernize its stance on key issues facing the nation and to revise its political strategy and tactics. And as was the case fifteen years ago, there are pervasive myths about the party's condition that stand in the way. Each contains a kernel of truth. But all have the effect of denying the need, and weakening the impetus, for fundamental change.

Myth is the operative word here. Any clouding of the mind has occurred in the author's reasoning and conjecture. The thwarting of change is spearheaded by the DLC. There is no Liberal Fundamentalism only the Liberal Ideal, which retains all of its original value and more. Mobilization is working; we, Liberals and Progressive Democrats, changed the conversation and now the reality of what to do about the War in Iraq. The Party has modernized out here in the real world far from academia and K Street (don't they have the Internet in DC yet?). Micro has overrun Macro in the fast changing world of media and political organizing.

Page 29

The Myth of Demography

This thesis claims that long-term, ongoing changes in the U.S. population will secure a Democratic majority for decades to come. Among the major components of this shift are: a growing class of post-industrial professionals; women (especially those who are single or highly educated) affected by the feminist revolution; and Hispanics and Asian immigrants, who have come to the United States in record numbers during the past generation. There is something to this thesis as well: Democrats are doing increasingly well among upscale professionals, and women as a whole remain more supportive of Democrats than Republicans, as do Hispanics. But there are some important trends that counterbalance these developments. As we show in an upcoming section of this paper on values, married women concerned about moral issues and security against terrorism have been moving away from national Democratic candidates, reducing John Kerry's margin among women to a scant 3 percentage points, compared to Bush's 11 point edge among men.

Moral values and security issues are the fog the "Republican Anarchy Collective" spewed out across the political landscape to hide the planned evisceration of the New Deal. The fact that the DLC not only fell for it but also then trumpeted it does not make it any more truthful. It' insidious to pronounce that security for women in America depends on the annihilation of Islamist Radicalism abroad while stripping them of their civil rights, under the banner of "morality", at home. It only proves that you can fool citizens drowning in fear and prejudice. Recent events however show Lincoln to have been prescient on how many times, whom and for how long the citizens can be misdirected.

Page 43

Having logged many presidential campaigns between us, the authors can attest to the fact that Democrats are likely to spend days on health care plans and minutes on character issues. (Republican campaigns do not often make such mistakes.) The delay in responding to the attacks of the Swift Boat Veterans will go down as one of the great strategic blunders of modern presidential politics. But the interplay between morality and personal characteristics raises a larger issue: in the public mind morality has as much to do with the personal integrity of the presidential candidates as it does with their stance on hot-button social issues. This presents Democratic candidates with an enormous strategic challenge. On the one hand, the public will notice—and mistrust — candidates who are perceived as changing their positions on issues that should be matters of firm conviction. On the other hand, the public will not accept candidates who forthrightly espouse moral views far outside the mainstream.

Morality as narrowly defined by duplicitous hucksters, outrageously removed from the religious traditions of tolerance, charity, inclusion, understanding, humility, forgiveness and peace is hollow and no more than the junk food of spiritual thought and belief (Pill-popping Rush Limbaugh, compulsive gambling Bill Bennett and wife-exchanging Newt Gingrich as the moral lions of the right beg incredulity). Gay marriage, women's reproductive rights and flag defamation are inflammatory themes designed to turn back the progress of the last 50 years made during the struggles for the right of privacy and personal freedom. Their sole aim is to deny citizens their civil-rights based on superstition, fear and hate. DLC regurgitation of these Lee Atwater poisons doesn't make them suddenly true. They remain the tools of the black arts of propaganda aimed at over-stimulated, insecure and paralyzed voters. Freedom still begins in the sanctity of your home and person.

Page 45

A recently completed series of focus groups among non-college rural and red state voters underscores the growing salience of morally laden cultural themes. Participants reported broad dissatisfaction with the Bush Administration on three issues—the lack of progress in Iraq, economic stagnation and job insecurity, and soaring health care costs—and indicated support for some progressive initiatives in these areas, which they believed Democrats would be more likely to offer. But as the summary of these focus groups goes on to note, "the introduction of cultural themes —specifically gay marriage, abortion, the importance of the traditional family unit, and the role of religion in public life — quickly renders [these progressive issues] almost irrelevant in terms of electoral politics at the national level." While participants see the Republican Party as offering a clear and consistent traditionalist stance on moral issues, they view Democrats as dangerously inconsistent on — or worse, as hostile to — traditional values: "Most referred to Democrats as 'liberal' on issues of morality, but some even go so far as to label them 'immoral,' 'morally bankrupt,' or even 'anti-religious'." They regard Democrats as too politically correct, as caring about the rights of the few rather than of the many. While this resistance might well have focused on racially tinged issues two decades ago, today it centers on religion and its role in public life. Issues such as removing the Ten Commandments from public building and outlawing public manger displays at Christmastime symbolize what these voters see as Democrats' support for an elitist "subversive minority" that is out to "erode the moral foundations of our country."

You would have to say that the greatest success of the Republican Anarchy Collective was the complete capitulation of the Democratic

Leadership Council to their bogus assumptions. Placing religious icons in public buildings cannot compare with the importance of a healthcare system that works for all citizens at a reasonable cost. Making it more important is the ultimate dog and pony show of modern policy manipulation. It is only surpassed by Wal-Mart being embraced by the consumers whose lives it is systematically destroying. Rather than standing up for the separation of church and state as the finest legal principle ever enacted to preserve religious freedom for all faiths, the DLC capitulated and shrank from the critical thinking necessary to provide a cogent policy argument to counter the RAC snake oil. Theocracy doesn't work. Ask the Iranians.

Page 49

At the same time, partisanship has become more intense, especially toward the ends of the ideological spectrum. More than three-quarters of liberals are critical of the Democratic leadership as failing to stand up for the party's traditional positions on key issues. At the same time, many religiously observant Americans, who tend to be conservative and Republican, have become less willing to search for common ground on key social issues. When asked whether "Even elected officials who are deeply religious sometimes have to make compromises and set their convictions aside to get results," only 63 percent of respondents who attend worship services at least once a week agreed, down from 82 percent in 2000. Evangelical Protestants and traditional Catholics both expressed an increased unwillingness to accept compromise, especially on issues such as abortion and gay marriage. The correlation between religious observance and political ideology is consistent and powerful: the more observant, the more conservative. For example, more than half of those who attend church once a week regard themselves as conservative, four times the percentage who are self-declared liberals.

Liberals and Progressives are leading voices in the new conversation that proclaims with constitutional provenance that, "the government is prohibited from interfering in matters of religious belief and religious institutions are prohibited from denying citizens any of their civil rights." We fought a revolution in 1776 to throw off the tyranny of the King and the "Church." A woman's right to choose when to reproduce is a "civil right." Every citizen's prerogative to wed whom they choose in a civil ceremony with all of the attendant rights granted therein and without the interference of any religious entity is a "civil right". Obviously, the battle for "rights reserved to the people" is not over.

Prejudice is not a platform to build a national party upon, unless you're a Republican. Let matters of faith be the domain of communities of faith and of families. Let matters of public policy be the domain of the constituted government without any restriction by religious dogma or intolerance. Discuss so-called "intelligent design" in the philosophy, theology or comparative religion classes if at all. Teach science in the science classes.

Page 53

> The lesson is clear. As the Great Sorting-Out intensifies, it will increase pressure on Democrats to appeal successfully to the center of the American electorate. By 2004, John Kerry was receiving so few conservative votes that he needed to get 60 percent of the moderate vote in order to win. To the extent that this polarization of American politics remains a stable feature of presidential elections, it means that Democrats will not win unless they are able to garner a substantial portion of the moderate vote — a direct challenge to the myth of mobilization that plays to "base" politics.

The "Myth of the Middle" has consumed the DLC for two decades. Now they are sidelined by their own success and its subsequent dead end. Leadership must necessarily offer an alternative to capitulation in order to empower voters to walk away from their fears and prejudices and develop a common sense of shared sacrifice.

Even the rich will do the right thing when we show them how the right thing will boost their bottom line; enlightened self-interest at work. A Progressive, Liberal future will be the product of offering Americans the choice of hard work leading to shared community reward and responsibility rather than easy emotional answers leading to division and decline. I'll take Roosevelt over Reagan any time.

Page 59

Along a number of dimensions, Liberals differ not only from other Democrats, but also from the country as a whole. Not only are they younger, better educated, and more prosperous; they are less likely ever to have been married or to have children in their home. They are more likely to be secular in their orientation, only half as likely as other Americans to attend religious services weekly, and only one third as likely to participate in Bible study or prayer groups. 61 percent of Liberals oppose displaying the Ten Commandments, versus only 22 percent of all Americans. A remarkable 80 percent of Liberals favor gay marriage; less than one third of their fellow Americans agree. In the area of defense and foreign policy, 67 percent of Liberals believe that the preemptive use of military force is rarely if ever justified, versus only 35 percent of all Americans. 65 percent favor cutting the defense budget to reduce the deficit; again, only 35 percent of the electorate would go along with them. Liberals are only half as likely to be military veterans as are Americans as a whole. Only two-fifths report that they regularly display the U.S. flag, versus two-thirds of their fellow citizens. While social issues and defense dominate today's political terrain, it is in these areas that Liberals espouse views diverging not only from those of other Democrats, but from Americans as a whole. To the extent that Liberals now constitute both the largest bloc within the Democratic coalition and the public face of the party, Democratic candidates for national office will be running uphill. Whatever their personal views, these candidates will be vulnerable to the kinds of negative campaigns that Republicans have proved adept at running since 1988. In current circumstances, it is hard to see how Democrats can overcome this disadvantage — unless candidates are willing and able to carry out their own suitably updated version of the strategy Bill Clinton so successfully employed in his 1992 primary and general election campaigns. Times change, of course. It is not hard to imagine two sets of circumstances that would reduce the salience of Democrats' difficulties on defense and social issues. In the first place, the Republicans could over-interpret the significance of their 2004 election victories and overreach in their use of the unchecked power they now enjoy. If they go too far — as they already have on a range of issues — they could end up abandoning the political center, offering new opportunities to their opposition. Second, as Americans continue to worry about their future in an increasingly competitive and rapidly changing global marketplace, the arena of political combat could shift back toward large economic issues. If so, the advantage shifts toward the Democrats, who are both more united on these issues than are Republicans and also more closely aligned with the electorate as a whole. But as Bill Clinton recognized, even in a year in which the economy is the dominant concern, candidates must pass the threshold of credibility on non-economic issues. This cannot happen unless they understand the problem they face and act boldly to address it.

The era of Bill Clinton has passed. It is up to history to judge its ultimate success or failure. Liberals and Progressives don't take a back seat to any political party or faction on any issue including, war, peace, economics, faith, governance or morality.

We are prepared to refocus the political debate of the Twenty First Century. We are prepared to offer America and the world the blueprint for the prosperous, inclusive, tolerant future humanity is struggling towards.

Modernity demands one of two outcomes. One is the way of totalitarianism the other is the path of democracy, political and economic. Standing for nothing and falling for everything with the DLC will only enhance the possibility of the former and add nothing to the latter.

Page 58

C. The Rise and Fall of The New Democrats

For most of the 1980s and 1990s, New Democrats struggled with traditional New Deal and post-1960s liberals to define the direction of their party. One of the key consequences of this struggle, coupled with the political strategy the Bush Administration chose to pursue, has been to blur many of the bright lines that once divided these factions. On the one hand, many liberals have accepted the logic of signature New Democratic themes such as fiscal restraint, balanced budgets, a generous immigration policy, and a more open world economy. On the other hand, the radical, unyielding conservatism of the Bush era has forced Democrats to subordinate their differences to the imperatives of mounting an effective opposition. In the 1990s, a majority of New Democrats would have supported the Central American Free Trade Agreement (CAFTA), and some would have stepped forward with their own Social Security reform plans. In 2005, by contrast, New Democrats in the House have opposed CAFTA almost unanimously, and New Democratic senators who were expected to break ranks on Social Security have refused to do so. The evidence supporting a new political alignment is more than anecdotal. Over the past two decades, the Pew Research Center for the People and the

Press has mapped the terrain of American politics, using sophisticated statistical methods to discover the typology of the electorate—that is, the basic groups into which they are divided. This technique makes it possible to examine the composition of party coalitions and to identify the characteristics of less partisan voters. During the 1990s, New Democrats emerged as a distinct ideological grouping. By 2005, they had all but disappeared as a separate group, while Liberals had grown to form the single largest group (19 percent of registered voters) within the core Democratic coalition. The authors of the Pew study suggest, "Some of the growth among Liberals comes from former New Democrats, whose views on national security and government regulation have become more polarized after more than four years of GOP control."

The outstanding problem of polls, statistics, focus groups and think tanks rooted in the stiff medium of academia, left or right, is that they are not on the street, in the field and searching for the flexible solutions to the problems of governance.

Like a mystic oracle, they will tell you whatever you want to hear and prove it with unending reams of research, for the right price. Pundits ensconced in the halls of power are driving the car of state by looking into the rear-view mirror instead of looking out of the windshield (thanks to Marshall McLuhan for that metaphor).

Research it all you want to but the speed of change is ramping up in an almost geometrical fashion. The DLC is not looking over the horizon. The DLC refuses to accept the end of the vertical era of leadership in favor of the new horizontal paradigm (thanks to Thomas Friedman for the flat world). Any policy that gives into superstition, fear, intolerance or blind greed is doomed, unless you want a world dominated by the Republican Anarchy Collective of debauched corporate pirates, delusional religious fanatics and sociopathic fringe dwellers.

Liberals and Progressives are on the verge of transforming the Democratic Party from bottom to top. The era of the DLC is passed. Maybe the reason these former New Democrats are once again Liberal and Progressive Democrats is simply that they woke up and realized that capitulation to bad policy for electoral expediency is never smart politics; it is ultimately self-defeating. If this is the case then welcome back to your principles.

To all the rest of the DLC, especially Ms. Kamarck and Mr. Galston, you've been triangulated. You are in fact Democrats with a conscience and the only place you fit with your principles intact is the Democratic Party with its Liberal Ideal, unless of course, you have crossed over and want to throw in with the Republican Anarchy Collective. I don't believe that you do.

I look forward to debating these ideas with any DLC, New Democrat, Third Way or Moderate Democrat. You have nothing to lose but your illusions. And you have everything to gain, like the support of Liberal and Progressive Democrats, for coming to your senses and joining us as we move America further, towards the realization of the original motto of the nation – E Pluribus Unum.

A Progressive Plan
(Towards a Progressive Majority in the Democratic Party)

Many members of the Progressive Caucus of the California Democratic Party (CDP) understand that more Caucus members and other Progressives must be elected as Delegates to the Democratic State Central Committee (DSCC) at the upcoming Assembly District (AD) Caucus elections and the next County Central Committee (CCC) elections. Progressives must be elected as Executive Board Representatives in particular from both of these bodies. Progressives must be elected to the Democratic National Committee (DNC) from California, which Executive Board Representatives will do in 2008, as officers of the CDP itself, which DSCC delegates will do in 2008 and as CCC members, which will happen in 2008 as well.

To this end, the Progressive Caucus calls upon Progressives throughout California to assist us in collecting Party election information, making it easily understood and widely distributed. As the vital first step in this process be aware that anyone wanting to vote or run for delegate to the DSCC, from the January 2007 AD Caucus elections, **MUST REGISTER AS A DEMOCRAT BEFORE OCTOBER 23rd**. Following that, we need your help in gathering information about the AD Caucus elections to be held the 2nd weekend in January. We need details about who is calling them, their contact information and where they will be held. That information is due by

December 1st to the CDP. As soon as we have this information, either from the Party or by our own efforts, we will then publish the information and distribute it statewide.

As a starting point for organizing this action, the Progressive Caucus proposes the following Plan to move towards a Progressive Majority in the CDP. With this information in hand the Progressive Movement will be empowered to gain voting majorities at every level of the California Democratic Party. With the election of Progressives as representatives and officers in the various levels of the CDP apparatus we will increase our power, implement Progressive policies and elect Progressive candidates in California and then across the nation.

Why a Progressive Plan?

Vast numbers of Democrats, past and present, have lost confidence in the Party leadership and direction. The Progressive Caucus of the California Democratic Party, in coalition with the broader Progressive community, intends to rectify this situation. Herein, we offer a Progressive Plan to accomplish just that.

Before we lay out the plan let us examine the Democratic Party as it now stands, why it should be and how it can be transformed. John Zogby noted in a recent column in the Huffington Post, (August 6, 2006), that discontented Democrats, now the majority of the Party, are in a mood to demand bold ideas and a return to principled leadership after the DLC led corporate crony policies of the last 20 years which have been a stupendous flop at the polls:

> *"...the Democrats will have a tough time convincing (Americans) that they are ready to take back control of Congress without offering any clarity on the Iraq War.*
>
> *Let's just look at the numbers from my [July 21] national poll. Overall, only 36% of likely voters told us that they agree that the war in Iraq has been "worth the loss of American lives", while 57% disagree. But the partisan splits are more revealing: only 16% of the Democrats polled said the war has been worth while 82% disagree and only 26% of Independents agree the war has been worth it while 72% disagree. On the Republican side, 64% said the war has been worth it, while 23% disagree. The war has been the principal cause of the nation's polarization in the past three years. The polling evidence shows the degree to which Iraq has become a Republican war. And these latest numbers are also noteworthy in that they show that about one in four Republicans have now pretty much given up on the war.*
>
> *All of which is to suggest that Democratic candidates will now probably be emboldened to take a stronger stance against the war. If principle doesn't win the day, at least the polling numbers are pretty clear what their base wants. Indeed, the polling numbers were pretty clear what Democrats and Independents wanted in 2004 - and the fact that they didn't receive the opposition to the war they were looking for*

from their standard-bearers is the main reason that they lost both the Presidency and did not pick up seats in either house of Congress."

Finding Our Progressive Voice

In the years following 2004 Progressives began mobilizing inside the Democratic Party. We achieved some notable successes including "Out of Iraq" resolutions across the nation. However, even with our rising strength, including the outcome of the Lamont-Lieberman Senate race in Connecticut, the Progressive Movement shouldn't be throwing confetti. Progressives lost most of the races they entered in the recent primaries. We were out-maneuvered by the entrenched political machine. We still don't have enough seats at the table of Democratic Party leadership to put the Party to work for our candidates. We have our work cut out for us.

Creating a Progressive Democratic Party

This political struggle is for "power," **political power** - the ability to persuade the voters and implement policy. It is a struggle between those who don't have it, those who do and the career politicians, electeds, appointeds and big donors who control it. Rather than being dispirited by the current state of affairs we should be motivated. It defines who we are and who we aren't, how we need to organize and what's at stake if we don't.

So, where do we go from here? We strategize, energize and organize the Progressive Movement. We take the Progressive Movement from outside of the Democratic Party into the Democratic Party. We form a coalition of all of the Progressive Movement's diverse national entities outside of the Party. We inform this coalition as to the why, where and how of our Progressive Plan for becoming the Progressive Majority inside the Democratic Party and together we make it happen.

Our hope is that many of those now arrayed against us will come to understand our principled positions and join us in reinvigorating the Liberal Ideal they once stood for, thereby, propelling the Democratic Party forward and enhancing the Party's social relevancy to the majority of working and middle class Americans. There is no justifiable neutral position in this epic search for the soul of the Democratic Party. The vote to adopt a neutral position on Clean Money Campaign Financing by the California Democratic Party was the center of contention at the most recent Executive Board meeting of the CDP this past August. Support for Clean Money, (Proposition 89), was defeated by a coalition of Democrats whose power to choose candidates and influence the party would be threatened by the passage of the proposition. This group included some union leaders (not rank & file members), electeds, consultants and big donors. They may think that this fight is over but their action to crush Clean Money has only provided all voters, no matter their partisan bias, the proof of its value and the impetus for making it happen.

We have been working on a broad outline of this Progressive Plan for the last year. We offer it here to all Progressive citizens working together to move the Democratic Party forward into the 21st Century. We believe that this can only be accomplished when Progressives are a voting majority at every level of the Democratic Party. Therefore, we are focusing our efforts on electing delegates to the State Central Committee, its Executive Board and the County Central Committees. If you read either your county's Democratic Party by-laws or the State Democratic Party by-laws they are clear as to when the delegates are elected. However, what is not clear, with regard to the Assembly District Caucus elections for delegates to the State Central Committee, is how many in total are elected, where they are elected in each particular AD, how and when names are put in nomination and the contact information for the person calling the meeting. Other than the fact that registered Democrats in primary elections elect delegates for County Central Committee, little information is known by the general public about the process or its importance in Party operations. Further, none of the processes at any level for becoming an appointed delegate are readily available nor is there a standard for appointment. This creates a situation where elected officials and leadership can control the outcome of Party votes by the number of appointed delegates regardless of the will of even an overwhelming majority of the Party membership.

A Progressive Call to Action

The Progressive Caucus calls upon Progressives throughout California to assist us in collecting Party election information, making it easily understood and widely distributed. With this information in hand the Progressive Movement will be empowered to gain voting majorities at every level of the Democratic Party.

Deteriorating living standards for working and middle class citizens, along with the outrageous appropriation of wealth and political power by the entrenched ruling elite have been the driving force behind our demand for change. However, the emotions of the last decade that propelled all of us to speak up and show up cannot create the changes we had hoped for by themselves. We must engage in the hard work of political organizing and working with others more effectively to achieve political gains within the Democratic Party. Our successes during the movements for Civil Rights, Against the Vietnam War and for Gender Equality were never translated into an ongoing political process and structure that would insure a Progressive American body politic. This cleared the way for the DLC, Neo-Liberals and moderate to conservative Democrats, to subvert the soul of the Democratic Party. We cannot afford to make the same mistake this time. We must move Progressive politics from the margin of the Democratic Party to the core of Party policy and action. With that in mind, we offer the following Plan.

Introduction to the Progressive Plan outline…

The first page of this outline lays out the basic elements of the Plan…

- A singular **goal** agreed upon by consensus
- An overarching **strategy** to achieve that goal
- A cohesive set of **tactics** to implement the strategy

That is followed by a brief explanation of the goal and an analysis of the current makeup of the Party. Next, a graphic shows the old paradigm of political power versus the new. The open exchange of ideas, available on the Internet, is inverting the "Pyramid of Power." Citizens are reclaiming, "the consent of the governed."

Page two is a cursory analysis of the elected and appointed members of both the government and the California Democratic Party at every level. These members all have voting privileges. In the Democratic Party, appointed members have if not a majority at least an equal number of votes. That is how the elected members, especially the leadership who do most of the appointing, maintain their power. The Party with a voting majority in each level of the government, local, state and federal, controls the floor of each body of the government and thereby the vote and the outcome of each vote. The wing of the Party in power that has the majority of the voting members in the Party at each level controls the floor of each body of the Party and thereby the vote, the outcome of the vote and the direction of the Party as well as the government. To effect change in

America we must control the vote in one political Party and make that Party the majority party in the government.

Page three starts with a brief outline of the upcoming electoral calendar both in the Democratic Party and in general elections. In order to move America in a Progressive direction we must first have a Democratic victory at the polls in November and take back the Federal legislature. However, that won't do us much good unless we follow it with a Progressive majority elected to the Democratic State Central Committee, which happens in January 2007 in each Assembly District caucus.

It is critical that every citizen who wishes to participate in that process as either a voting member of the Assembly District caucus or who wants to run for delegate to the DSCC from those Assembly District caucuses *MUST REGISTER AS A DEMOCRAT FOR THIS NOVEMBER ELECTION: BEFORE OCTOBER 23rd*. We have included a proposed coalition meeting of the Progressive Movement in 2007. This would probably be most effective in the fall of 2007 and include representation of all of the Progressive Caucuses in each state's Democratic Party plus representative's of the major national Progressive organizations. No electeds will be allowed to campaign there and no celebrities invited to opine. We should concentrate on group inter-working and refining the Plan as to strategy and tactics. To be effective this meeting should be less talk and more walk.

Finally under tactics we have assembled what we know about the make-up of the various governing bodies of the CDP. As you can see the appointed members control the balance of power. So, we need precise information as to the how, when and where of becoming the electeds so we can then do the appointing and achieve a Progressive Majority of voting members in the Democratic Party.

Following this explanation is the outline of the Progressive Plan: a starting document. We encourage everyone's input and participation. However, time is of the essence. These electoral cycles are ongoing and we need to be prepared for each one and then the next and the next. This process of creating a Progressive Liberal Democratic Party and America will not be easy. It will span at least a decade. Liberals, who we believe are the new center in the Democratic Party, are our natural allies in this endeavor. DLC-Moderates are our opposition but in the spirit of "recycling," which we embrace, we should leave an open door for them to join us when they come home to their principles. We are often asked, "Who is a Progressive?" We offer this guideline: A Democrat is any citizen who votes for Democratic Party candidates. A Liberal is any citizen who believes in the Liberal Ideal as espoused by Americans for over two centuries (e.g. favoring proposals for reform, open to new ideas for progress, and tolerant of the ideas and behavior of others; broad-minded). A Progressive is any citizen who is actively promoting the Liberal Ideal in the political process. However, before action can commence a Progressive must have an understanding of the historical analysis of the prevailing social construct and socio-economic reality as it relates to those who are systematically disenfranchised. With that shared view the Progressive Movement can unite Progressive citizens to create a coalition that brings transformative political policy back into the Democratic Party.

The Progressive Caucus Platform, 2006

The Progressive Caucus of the California Democratic Party has formulated four policy areas to concentrate on at this time. They are in brief:

1 – **Out of Iraq**
   - Immediate withdrawal and
       renunciation of preemptive war
2 – **Universal Healthcare**
   - Single-payer healthcare for all Americans
3 – **Election Integrity**
   - Election Protection
       (Count every vote as cast)
   - Clean Money
       (Public financing of campaigns)
4 – **Living Wage**
   - Not merely a minimum wage

If you agree that these are priority policy issues among the many serious issues of the day then you are a Liberal. If you are actively working to make them happen then you are a Progressive.

Even we though we all may differ as to the nuance of our solutions to these and other problems facing society we must overcome our personal investment in our own ideas and create a consensus that is put into action. We must join with our natural allies, Liberal Democrats, and even though we may know many Democrats who are right wing or cooperating with Republicans and Establishment power brokers we must remain inclusive and welcome them back to their principles as well. As we sweep the DLC cabal from office and the Democratic Party we should leave open the possibility of growth for every Democrat. Our Progressive Plan begins in California, proceeds to every state in the union, and culminates in a Progressive Democratic National Committee. Join with us. Your democracy depends on your participation.

Now is the Time. This is the Place. We are the People.

Stand Up. Show Up. Speak Up.

Signed by:

The Officers of the Progressive Caucus of the California Democratic Party

**Mal Burnstein   Mayme Hubert
Jeffrey Killeen   Dotty LeMieux
Narges Niedzwiecki
Jo Olson   Ahjamu Makalani
Brad Parker   Joye Swan**

Progressive Plan - Progressive Voice - Progressive Action

Progressive Liberal Democrats must have the three essential elements of politics clearly defined for the Progressive Movement to make the transition from outside of the Democratic Party to inside. Those elements are:

- A singular **goal** agreed upon by consensus
- An overarching **strategy** to achieve that goal
- A cohesive set of **tactics** to implement the strategy

To form a majority in the Democratic Party, Progressive Democrats must align with the new center, Liberals, to wrest control of the Party from DLC Moderates who are the new Right Wing of the Democratic Party.

Progressive – Liberal – DLC Moderate

GOAL

In order to form a more perfect Union, Progressive and Liberal Democrats must *Strategize, Energize and Organize* the Democratic Party at every level. Only then will a Progressive Liberal Democratic government come into being in America.

Pyramid of Power

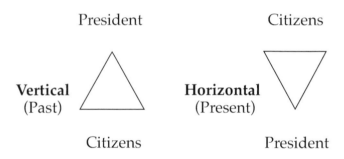

Political power rests in the citizens who are elected or appointed (selected) to seats in the leadership of political parties (i.e. voting members) and in citizens who are elected or appointed to official offices at the various levels of government.

Government	Elected	Appointed
Federal		
- Executive	X	X
- Legislative	X	
- Judicial		X
State		
- Executive	X	X
- Legislative	X	
- Judicial	X	X
County/Parrish		
- Executive	X	X
- Legislative	X	
- Judicial	X	X
City		
- Executive	X	X
- Legislative	X	X
- Judicial	X	X

Democratic Party	Elected	Appointed
DNC		
- Executive	X	X
- Legislative (members)	X	X
- Ex Officio (Superdelegates)		X
State (CDP)		
- Executive	X	X
- Legislative (Central Committee)	X	X
- Ex Officio (Superdelegates)		X
- Executive Board	X	X
County		
- Executive	X	X
- Legislative	X	X
- Ex Officio (Superdelegates)		X
City		
- Executive	X	X
- Legislative	X	X
- Ex Officio (Superdelegates)		X

STRATEGY

Timeline

- **2008 Nov. General Election**
- 2008 Democratic Convention
- **2008 CDP Convention**
- 2007 Progressive Movement Coalition Meeting
- **2007 CDP Convention**
- **2007 Jan. AD Elections**
- **2006 Nov. General Election**

TACTICS

CDP – Democratic State Central Committee

Approx. **2826** members
- **960** (elected by ADs)
- **933** (elected by CCCs)
- **933** (includes nominees {& their appointees}, electeds {& their appointees}, State Party Officers {& their appointees}, DNC members

County Central Committees

Size differs with each County
- Most elected from ADs?
- Others serve ex officio (appointed)

CDP Executive Board

Approx. **314** -?
- **80** (elected by ADs)
- **104** (elected by CCCs)
- **35** Committee Chairs (appointed)
- ?? Includes DNC, State Constitutional Officers, State Party Officers, Caucus Chairs

(Submitted to and passed by the membership of the Progressive Caucus of the CDP in October 2006)

Additional editing by:
Jo Olson, Joye Swan,
Mayme Hubert, Dotty LeMieux

now is the time...

Part II

Futuring The
California Democratic Party

2005 Out of Iraq CDP Convention Speech

April 2005

I'm Brad Parker from the 41st AD, Valley Democrats United and the Progressive Democrats of America. I rise in support of the Iraq resolution, 45A, as written.

California is the Conscience of the Nation.

The California Democratic Party should be the Conscience of the Democratic National Party.

That is why I urge you, my fellow delegates, to support this resolution, the third highest resolution in votes counted.

Over 100 Americans have died in Iraq since the much bally-hooed election, which has failed to form a government.

American corporations are building Water and Power plants with the instructions on them written in English not Arabic. They don't know where they are but we know where they are.

We must send a message. You my fellow delegates have the opportunity to do what the Congress has failed to do, with the exception of members like Barbara Lee and Lynn Woolsey from California, and support HR35.

This is only the beginning in a long struggle. We have, a long road ahead of us, much, much further to go.

I urge all the delegates to pass this resolution, today.

The Whole World is Watching.

TREMORS INSIDE THE CDP:
Grassroots Activists Come Together
To Transform The California Democratic Party

April 2005

On the afternoon of Sunday, April 17th, 2005, tremors were felt at the Los Angeles Convention Center. It wasn't Mother Earth rumbling the building but the political descendents of Mother Jones, who were inside at the California Democratic Party Convention and were ready to rumble. However, that was merely the culmination of a statewide surge of activism that began many years earlier.

For the past 13 years, Democrats in California and around the country have suffered mounting losses at the polls. After the exuberance of Bill Clinton's 1992 victory came the rising defeats in the Congress. Both houses were lost in short order. Then came the ignominious selection of Bush by the U.S. Supreme Court in 2000. That was followed by the 2003 recall of Gray Davis and election of Arnold Schwarzenegger to the statehouse in California. Oh yes, and the 2004 re-selection of "W" only rubbed salt into the wounds. From these defeats, a phoenix rose in California that would bring a not so subtle twist of fate to the California Democratic Party; "Grassroots Activism" on a level not seen since the Vietnam War era and the United Farm Workers movement gained momentum and instead of rallying against Republicans, is squarely aimed at transforming the California Democratic Party.

From across the state, beginning after the 2004 election, grassroots activists, who had put their heart and soul into electing Sen. John Kerry, gathered in every precinct in the state. Instead of going home in defeat, they decided to come together to create the type of permanent change needed to transform the political landscape. Some went to work outside the party. Others decided that the key to a new political reality in America was a new Democratic party. Many activists believed that the stranglehold of the Democratic Leadership Council had caused the DNC to drift towards the shoals of moderate irrelevancy and had finally grounded the party in the shifting sands of, "Better to Stand for Nothing than to Lose on Principle". Grassroots activists in California were determined to end the era of "Republican Lite" DNC and CDP political equivocating.

In Democratic Clubs, Assembly District Committees and chapters of National Progressive Organizations, activists planned, campaigned and then moved into the ranks of the CDP. An astonishing 35% of all the delegates to the 2005 convention in Los Angeles were from the grassroots. New faces with little patience for the old games had arrived to make a difference. They brought with them over 90 proposed resolutions to make the voice of the grassroots heard at the top of the party. Responding to organizing and pressure from every corner of the state the CDP even allowed a "Progressive Issues Coalition" meeting, aimed at forming a progressive caucus within the party.

Friday began with the PIC meeting and down the

hall the Resolutions committee meeting among others. Delegates were jamming both rooms to capacity. The Progressive caucus was brought forward at the convention by; Joye Swan, Mal Burnstein, Dotty LeMieux, Mark Hull-Richter, Mayme Hubert, Jo Olson and Ruth Hull-Richter among others. Temporary officers were elected but CDP elected officials, coming in to give little more than campaign speeches, steadily interrupted all other business that could have been done. This tradition at the convention was a waste of valuable organizing time for all caucuses who allowed it. However, even the presence of this meeting at the convention was a success for all progressives; given that many officers of the party and members of the CDP Executive Board were opposed to its formation. At this time, the fate of the "Progressive Caucus" is still unknown, given that those forces opposed to it would just like everyone to shut up and go home. Down the hall though, the meeting of the Resolutions committee would prove to be the first crack in the staid foundation of the CDP.

Of the 90 plus resolutions, 12 were about the "War In Iraq." The "Iraq" resolutions were brought to the convention after being sponsored and adopted by Assembly District Committees, Democratic Clubs, County Central Committees and Local Chapters of national progressive organizations from all over California. Much to her credit, Rep. Maxine Waters is also on the list of sponsors. After debate and votes of the committee had determined that there would be an "Iraq" resolution, the work turned to what the language of the resolution would be. Opinions varied widely from immediate withdrawal to more moderate proposals for timetables and strategies extending off into the future. Final language was approved and a vote was scheduled for the Saturday afternoon meeting. Before the meeting, a hastily called ad hoc meeting of progressive activists took place that would prove crucial to the ultimate passage of the resolution.

Fortunately for all California grassroots activists, Tim Carpenter, national director of Progressive Democrats of America, was on hand to lay out a strategy that would prove to be successful at both the Saturday Resolutions Committee meeting and the Sunday floor vote. Tim is a long time grassroots activist who had served in the CDP, so he was familiar with many of the committee members and most importantly, he knew all of the parliamentary procedures that must be followed to get a resolution through. He pointed out that of the 30 left for consideration perhaps only 10 would make the final report. We all wanted the "Iraq" resolution to be one of those. He knew there would only be one speaker allowed to speak on behalf of the final "Iraq" resolution at the committee meeting. I was nominated and then chosen by a vote of the ad hoc committee and I drafted a short, concise speech. Tim told everyone to stand up when I was speaking to show the committee the depth of support. At the meeting, we stood up, I spoke, we cheered and the "Iraq" resolution passed with the third highest number of votes. However, down the hall, DNC Chair Howard Dean was speaking and failed to even mention the war in an otherwise notable speech. Fissures were unsettling the foundation of the

CDP and reaching even to the DNC.

On Sunday the struggle for passage of the "Iraq" resolution took several dramatic turns. Inola Henry, who chaired all of the Resolutions Committee meetings, once again showed her fairness, impartiality and thorough understanding of all procedures involved in running a committee meeting during the closing session. I was signed up to be one of two speakers allowed to speak from the floor in support of the "Iraq" resolution when Tim Carpenter came up and said that there were behind the scenes efforts underway to get the resolution, in fact all resolutions, killed under the provision that if any were pulled from the report to be debated, a call for a quorum would be made and if no quorum existed then all of the measures would be held over until the next Executive Board meeting of the CDP Central Committee. Tim advised everyone not to pull the resolution for discussion. Many delegates wanted to amend, or strengthen or even water down the resolution but all agreed to let it stand as written and have an up or down vote with all of the 15 adopted resolutions that made it to the floor. Suddenly, a delegate in opposition pulled the resolution. Supporters were scrambling to get to the mike to speak. Tim, with other delegates, got the Chair to recognize that there was in fact a quorum and to state that there was a quorum from the podium and for the record. Now, all we needed was a majority vote. The opposition spoke first and then I rose to speak and began, "California is the conscience of the nation… the California Democratic Party should be the conscience of the Democratic National Party…

Send a message..." We all stood together and made a noise that sent a tremor through the establishment of the CDP. Over 2000 delegates voted in favor with one vote against. Our resolution passed with all of the other 15 resolutions and the CDP was put on notice that the grassroots is here to stay.

Grassroots activists from liberal to progressive, from every county, brought a strong and passionate voice back to the CDP. Resolutions against CAFTA, for Clean Money Elections and a host of progressive issues were passed. Yet, there remain many in the CDP and the DNC who fear taking a strong stand on principle. They prefer to nuance all issues to the middle of nowhere. Focus group and pollster driven with a fear of not being re-elected, they stand with the Republican Party and deny the great Liberal tradition of the Democratic Party from the time of Franklin Delano Roosevelt to the Great Society. Their interests lie at the door to the country club, not at the door to the future of the country. Lobbyists and campaign contributors have their ear, not "we the people." They are good people maintaining a bad system, even in the CDP and the DNC. Grassroots activists represent the bottom-up approach to governance that is sorely lacking in an American top-down political system that is failing the citizens, alive and yet to be born.

So, we did some historic things at this convention but much remains to be done. For a start we need to clear the air on a couple of issues resulting from work leading up to the convention and during it. There is dissension, even anger in the ranks of progressives following our success. Some people who were part of the original planning for a "Progressive Caucus" were dropped from the organizing committee during the formation process. Others were never informed of the process. Many of these activists feel that the process was exclusive in the least and un-democratic at best. Delegates from all over the state feel that people and organizations, local, state and national, are taking credit for the passage of the resolutions who don't deserve it. Some delegates thought that my election to speak for the "Iraq" resolution was un-democratic, planned or irrelevant.

For all of us who participated, from the precinct level to the floor of the convention, thousands of us in California, credit where credit is due; "WE DID IT." It took all of our efforts to accomplish even this good beginning. I'm sure the people who formed the "Progressive Caucus" committee had everyone's best interest in mind and were not attempting to exclude anyone from getting to the front of the room. I can assure you that Tim Carpenter was there to guide us in the process and bring it to a successful conclusion as a progressive grassroots activist and concerned citizen, not the director of Progressive Democrats of America. For my part, I was there in solidarity with all of you, not as member of Progressive Democrats of Los Angeles. Many delegates could have given those speeches in support that I gave and done a very good job at that. It was an honor for me to do so. I look forward to supporting as many of you as possible with the opportunity to do the same. We are all rightly proud of the groups that we represent but should be even more proud of what we all can accomplish together. People in power who do not want us to succeed are giddy with laughter at the mention of our internal strife.

Republicans and scared Democrats are counting on us not being able to organize and galvanize this progressive movement. Status quo politicians in all parties are betting that we fall apart in bitter feuds over who is getting credit and who is leading the parade. We have met the enemy and the only enemy we have is - US. I didn't go to the convention to grab the spotlight. I'm sure you didn't either. Each one of us played an important part; delegates, volunteers and observers, no person's actions were irrelevant. I don't give a damn who is at the front of the room. However, I will loudly condemn any trivialization of our movement into name-calling and in-fighting that destroys this cause. Let me say it again, "WE" did this. We sent a message. Those tremors that rocked the party were generated by all of "US." Proof of just how much we shook up the CDP and the DNC - you can't find any of the Resolutions that were passed, especially the "Iraq" resolution, on the CDP or DNC websites, or any comment at all by any official of the Party.

To all of the members of the CDP and DNC who are opposed to this reawakening of our political conscience, I say, "don't waste your good time and energy." You should be with us and Sen. Barbara Boxer and Rep. Barbara Lee and Rep. Lynn Woolsey and Rep. Maxine Waters and all Progressive Liberal Democrats and the many others across the state of California and the nation who are transforming the Democratic Party. Grassroots activists are growing a new political landscape from the bottom up to the top. That's not an earthquake cracking the moribund foundations of the CDP and the DNC; it's leaves of grass coming up through the concrete to reinvigorate the political process. The California Democratic Party has become the conscience of the nation. "WE," grassroots activists, did it!

Brad Parker
Vice Chair, Progressive Democrats of Los Angeles
Valley Democrats United
CDCC Delegate, 41st AD (Alt. to the EB)
Democratic Party of the San Fernando Valley
CA-27th Congressional District (Brad Sherman)
CA-41st Assembly District (Fran Pavley)
CA-21st State Senate District (Jack Scott)

Progressives Embraced by the CDP

August 2005

Over the weekend of July 29th to 31st, in Sacramento, California, the California Democratic Party officially recognized the Progressive Caucus. Thousands of Democratic Party activists from all over the state had worked and organized to make this a reality.

Many thanks are in order. First to the Interim Board, Jo Olson, Mal Burnstein, Joye Swan, Jeffrey Killeen, Mayme Hubert, Ahjamu Makalani, Narges Niedzwiecki and Stan West. They stayed on top of the procedure and provided the Executive Board with all of the necessary filings and by-laws that the board needed to make an informed decision. They also spoke eloquently at the rules committee hearing. Thanks to all of them for their leadership. Then to the CDP Party leadership, Senator Art Torres, Reginald Byron Jones-Sawyer, Alicia Wang, Alexandra Gallardo-Rooker, Bob Mulholland and most importantly Garry Shay. Chairman Torres and the leadership proved to be true to their Progressive roots and made this success possible from within the CDP. Garry Shay was especially helpful and supportive as the Rules Committee Chair. Thanks to all of them for their openness and leadership.

However, the greatest thanks should go to the unnamed thousands of Grassroots Activists from around the state who provided the impetus behind this movement. Not only the new activists who jammed the rooms at the CDP convention and Executive Board meetings but to those who have been in the CDP for decades, providing leadership on all of the Progressive issues, so important to the rank and file Democrats. To all of the unnamed individuals who worked and campaigned for this without commendation goes our deepest bow.

The Progressive Caucus meeting at the E. Board weekend was contentious, which is to be expected with such a spirited group. Natasha Hull-Richter was not allowed to retain her seat on the board because the rules of the Party allow only qualified registered voters to sit on caucus boards and she is not yet of voting age. It was an unavoidable oversight, which caused a lot of misunderstanding. Nonetheless, the Hull-Richter family played an important part in the formation of the caucus and we look forward to their vital contributions in the future. Some comments about elected Democrats from the state caused a great commotion. After a heated debate, it was agreed that the decorum necessary for an official body of the CDP mandates policy discussions as wide ranging and open as possible but does not and should not permit partisan personality or character assessment. Critiques of policy are vital to the Party but critiques of personalities at CDP meetings are counter-productive and divisive. Also, long time Progressive activists chided the current crop of activists just joining the CDP leadership for not reaching out to them. It was an overdue and warranted reminder that this movement wasn't born yesterday and that the leadership of the Progressive Caucus needs people from every era of Progressive activism.

On a personal note, I would like to thank everyone for overcoming the passion of the moment and taking the first steps toward trust and cooperation. We each have our part to play in this Party. Great ideas are vital to our direction and stoke the fires of political action. Leadership at every level must practice the fine arts of inclusion and fairness. Lively debate is our tool for developing our cohesion, strategy and tactics. But in the end, as Eric Bauman of the LACDP has stated, getting Democrats elected is our job and our goal. Yes, we need the Progressive Caucus to push for the ideals of all Democrats but we need to get Democrats with those ideals "elected" or we are nothing more than a debate society.

So, join those of us who are members of the new Progressive Caucus of the California Democratic Party and let's get to work and change this state, this nation, our world, one idea and one election after another. California is the conscience of the nation and the California Democratic Party is the conscience of the national Democratic Party.

California Democrats: Preserve the Ads

September 2005

As you all know, the by-laws of the CDP are being re-written. As this has proceeded, many questions have arisen as to the intent and effect of the revision. Under the terms of the BCRA (McCain-Feingold Act), strict guidelines have been implemented for all political parties regarding most aspects of political activity; especially the raising of money and all of the many expenditures that money can be used for. The CDP is revising its by-laws in order to be in line with those guidelines, among other issues, as it should.

However, it is the belief of many Grassroots Activists that the new entities envisioned in the proposals, replacing current Assembly District Committees, which have been sent forth from the committee drafting the revision, fall short of providing for adequate procedures guaranteeing Activists a voice in the policy decisions of the Party. In other words, there is widespread belief that the proposals will deny Activists access to policy decisions of the CDP.

There are many reasons for this assumption. First - there is the question of who chose the group doing the revision? Was the entire general body of Delegates, Regional Directors and other elected interested parties advised of this impending revision and asked for input at the beginning of the process? Is the revision merely to make the CDP more money friendly and top down oriented or to bolster the Grassroots Activists and their "ideas" as well? Finally, what function should the Assembly District Committees have in overall Party elections, policy and organization?

For many of us who are active at the AD, club and local level, the recent convention in Los Angeles was an eye-opener. Together, activists from all over the state brought forward and passed 15 resolutions clearly defining the policy positions of a majority of Democrats in California. Resolutions, calling for a withdrawal from Iraq, strengthening Social Security, Clean Money Campaigns and much more, received the enthusiastic vote of the majority of delegates at the convention. New Grassroots Activists, comprising 35% of all delegates, organized with progressive leaders and returning delegates to make this bold statement of principle.

However, after the convention, the resolutions were not posted on the CDP web site or released to the press. After a campaign, "Publish The Resolutions," led by Valley Democrats United (a San Fernando Valley Democratic Club) the resolutions were eventually posted deep in the back pages of the CDP web site.

Activists are asking why the CDP was slow to respond and to this day have not put a link to the resolutions on the home page or sent a letter from the Chair or the Congressional delegation or the state elected officials acknowledging the contribution of the Grassroots Activists to the policy decisions of the Party. This lack of communication and acknowledgement is one of the roots of the dissension surrounding the proposed revision.

If you talk to long time Party activists from across the state, you will discover another source of disagreement. In some parts of the state, AD committees are very active and provide for the most direct access to the CDP on all matters of candidates, campaigns and most importantly, policy (i.e. Resolutions and Platform). In some parts of the state, AD committees are not run on an inclusive and open basis. In too many parts of the state, AD committees are not functioning at all. In other Ads, clubs are more important. In still others, County Central Committees take a leading role. The question is; how do we define the revised structure of the CDP and take in these divergent realities?

Where AD committees are exclusive or non-functioning, it is understandable that CDP members would want them abolished. However, for a substantial percentage of CDP members, the AD committees are the center of issues, ideas and resolutions and they want them maintained. Again the question is; what new AD organization will work the best and comply with BCRA? More importantly, for many Grassroots Activists across the state the question is; how will the AD revision strengthen the voice of the Grassroots Activists in policy decisions in the future when it appears they are being ignored today?

I believe in the leadership of Garry Shay in this matter. I have found him to be open to comment and ideas. Garry and Coby King have been traveling the state to explain their analysis of the situation. While I have not always agreed with Garry's conclusions, I feel confident in his intent. I'm positive that he wants to provide for a more inclusive party that responds not only to large money donors and incumbents but also to the true strength of the Party - the Grassroots Activists. All Democrats, from the bottom to the top of the Party, must find a way to work together to achieve the results we are dedicated to - social justice, equality, opportunity and so much more. Garry is conducting a conversation, a dialogue, of the utmost importance as we proceed as a Party. He deserves our praise for the Democratic nature of his inquiry. But even more importantly, he and Coby and the revision committee need our input.

For my part, I can see how two separate entities, one for delegate election and one for campaigns and candidates can work. However, if one or both doesn't have a solid, easily explainable and inclusive mechanism for the policy contributions of Grassroots Activists, then the entire enterprise will fall flat. I can only support a new CDP that solves the problem experienced by the thousands of Democrats, from across California, who feel disenfranchised by the leadership ignoring the policy and principles embodied in the 15 resolutions passed at this year's convention. Garry Shay understands this and I am confident he will continue working until Grassroots Activists are guaranteed a voice and access in the new CDP By-Laws. Intent alone is not sufficient. Inclusion must be the final effect.

So, if you have thoughts and contributions that you want to add to this vital process, I encourage you to do so and do so now. If you can attend the CDP Executive Board meeting Friday, July 29th to Sunday July 30th, at the Radisson Hotel in Sacramento, do so. The meetings are open to all Democrats. The Rules Committee meets on Saturday. They are the committee in charge of the revision. If you can't attend email your comments to Robert Jordan.

Any revision that doesn't address the concerns of the Grassroots Activists will not empower the leadership. No one denies the importance of our elected officials, major contributors or CDP leadership but they are powerless without the Grassroots Activists. It will do nothing but good to strengthen the Grassroots, acknowledge their contribution and listen to their policy positions. The best ideas are coming from the bottom of the policy pyramid. There is a reason that nearly 50% of eligible voters do not vote. They don't have a voice in policy. They don't have a stake in the process. Incumbency appears to be the only principle that the CDP and the DNC are willing to fight for. The only call or email most Democrats get is to ask for money not ideas. To change that perception, the leadership must create access and relevancy for the people who do the phone banking, precinct walking and most importantly vote and put Democrats in office. Garry Shay knows this. You should let him know that you know it as well. California is the conscience of the nation. The California Democratic Party should reflect and enable that conscience.

this is the place...

The Rumble in River City

May 2006

"One woman of courage is a majority." That was part of the speech in support of Marcy Winograd that I was honored to be able to deliver at the California Democratic Party Convention in Sacramento. In paraphrasing Max Cleland's remarks, which preceded the final statewide endorsement vote, I could have also included the sentence, "and 'WE', the Progressive Movement, are the majority of this Party as well." But first let me recall the highlights of the convention and congratulate the coalition who made them possible. There was the Impeachment Forum, organized by the Progressive Caucus of the CDP and supported by Sacramento for Democracy. Military Families Speak Out, IVAW, Code Pink, Veterans for Peace, After Downing Street, DFA and PDA all played a part at the forum and throughout the convention. Platform committee meetings were well attended and featured members of the Progressive Movement, from across the state, who successfully put much needed progressive language into the CDP platform. PDA's table was a center for Progressive Activist's information and gathering. PDA's hospitality suite sparked more calls for action and included, Rev. Lenox Yearwood, Tim Carpenter and Mimi Kennedy among others. Inside the Party annual confab, the most closely watched race was the Winograd campaign. The noble effort to uphold democracy and challenge incumbency fell just short of the votes needed to deny Jane

Harmon and the DLC wing of the Party an unwarranted endorsement. The citizens decide on June 6th and that result will be markedly different. The vote on the floor proved that, with focused organizing based on principled ideas, next year the Progressive Movement will be the majority of the delegates and the carcass of the Democratic Party will once again be a caucus we can all be proud of.

COUNT ME OUT

May 2006

WOW… now that was a season of darkness, wasn't it? Have you ever been witness to, let alone participant in, such a spectacle of bad intentions masquerading as representative governance? Why you would have to go to City Hall or the State Capitol or Congress to find a rival flimflammery. In fact, that's the genesis of this enforcement process. Oh excuse me, I meant to say endorsement process.

Like a tawdry pimp ginning up the Johns and Ho's, it glided from hood to hood in its flashy trashy vehicle spewing its silent killer fumes over the somnambulant crowd. Narrow self-interest is very seductive, even to those of us vigilantly exorcising it from our modus operandi in favor of enlightened self-interest. One way or the other self-interest is part of our DNA. Like sleeping Buddhas, we can awaken but only if we abandon our primal instruction to always make our narrow self-interests primary in our pursuits. We have to become aware of our actions and meditate upon the possibilities of the group responsibilities above our own, so that we can grow into enlightened self-interest. It's no easy walk to freedom. But I digress.

Tammany Hall types in fact invented endorsement over a century ago to strong-arm constituents into toeing the line. It's a gangster process replete with thugs and bosses whirling around from meeting to meeting making sure you support their handpicked stooge. This is then foisted upon the vertiginous multitude as the "choice of the people." It's a scene out of the "Sopranos" not Philadelphia in "1776". Right now, you're probably thinking that you weren't involved in that but you would be wrong, we are all complicit. Sometimes you liked the outcome and boasted that it was principled. Sometimes you decried the outcome and said it was rigged. In fact, a very few were principled but the overwhelming majority were rigged. Coercion, innuendo, character assassination, threats, strong-arm tactics and banana republic style manipulation of appointed delegates along with secret society style recommendation committees rigged them. Ouch, is this the Da Vinci code in our midst? No, it is worse. It's dupes being duped. It's a three card Monte swindle by a bunch of grifters. I'm not talking about us, the peons. I'm talking about the patrons.

Corporate Cronies need a rigged system to keep the deception of representative government from being uncovered. In their narrow self-interest, they have rigged every level of government to appear to be controlled by the vote, when in fact; it is manipulated by the money. What better way to keep all of the dogs in the kennel than to train them at an early age? Voila, the endorsement process. First you have enforcement, I meant to say endorsement, at the local level, Assembly Districts, clubs and chapters of national organizations. Then you repeat the indoctrination at the County Central Committee level and finally take it to the State level (I should say that the

Federal Auction is actually the big enchilada) where any result not completed at lower levels can be institutionally guaranteed with clever rules and voluminous pronouncements and testimonials by the leadership. Plus, the people are deceived into believing they had a choice because a vote is taken. Sweet, huh? All the while the leadership is lining up those lucrative new lobbying jobs being offered by the "Candyman" (i.e. Corporate sponsors) that will help them make a soft landing into retirement. If you can't see this happening, then I must assume that you are angling for a position in the leadership, as it is currently constituted, rather than making the effort to wake up and challenge the corporate plantation masters.

Perhaps, the saddest chapter of this most recent saga drenched in sludge was the spectacle of Progressive friends clutching their long knives to deny each other one of these meaningless prizes. Principled players slugged it out in a fiesta of self-immolation. I presided over one of these trivialities blown up by bogus imaginary rewards and witnessed good people caught in a bad system, as Tom Hayden has remarked, marching determinedly into a ditch of exasperated hollowed out grimness. What a waste.

Perhaps, the iconic zenith of this symphony of mendacity was the vote on the floor of the CDP convention on Sunday morning April 30th. Marcy Winograd's contest for endorsement with Jane Harmon pitted the Progressive Movement against the DLC machine. On an almost purely factional vote, Jane and the hackocracy prevailed with a

65% to 35% vote. That same 65% had stood with the 35% just a year before, as we repudiated the leadership and the Bush administration with our Withdrawal From Iraq resolution. Here the 65% was, betraying their conscience to endorse the "best Republican the Democrats have ever had." Jane Harmon, the ultimate Right-Wing War Hawk, prevailed, eviscerating any vestige of moral high ground the 65% had left. Even Antonio Villaraigosa had sold out his Progressive base and sent a letter, placed on every chair on the floor, begging the delegates to support Jane. Somewhere a mother was weeping at a funeral in Iraq or America but the Democratic Party machine rolled on.

For my part, I will never again participate in the endorsement process. Further, I will do everything in my power to organize against the process in every organization I am a member of. I refuse to be manipulated into Hobbesian choices by the Corporate vultures picking at the bones of the Republic. I am proud to be a member of Valley Democrats United, which steadfastly refuses to hold one of these chicaneries. I am equally proud to have not been endorsed by any organization in my Los Angeles County Central Committee race. I leave it to the people, the citizens, and the voters to decide my fate in that race. Win or lose, I can live with the outcome of their choice. What I cannot live with is this divisive, maniacal, arcane, insidious, vituperative and undemocratic banana republic circus of so-called endorsement, which stands for enforcement and makes a thinking caring person want to vomit. I'll have to take many showers to get the foul stench of this process off of me. How about you?

Got Soul?

May 2006

Democrats,

The debate for the Soul of the Party has boiled over into a shouting match. Read this article from the Washington Post:

http://www.washingtonpost.com/wp-dyn/content/article/2006/05/10/AR2006051001927.html?referrer=emailarticle

The old Liberals vs. Dixiecrats squabble, is now the Progressives vs. DLC Moderates debacle. On the DLC, DCCC and DSCC side are the Establishment Dems led by Rahm Emanuel and Chuck Schumer. They are the attack dogs as DNC Chair Howard Dean discovered. As the last vestiges of the DLC/Clinton machine grasp to power, they are doing everything possible to derail the Progressive Movement's steady transformation of the Party they once controlled. Even though he may not represent some Progressive Democrat's idea of a leader, Howard Dean is the focus of their current fight for control of the Party. Why? They say it is because he has instituted a 50 state plan.

"We need to be a national Party again, and I think we have to run on a message that can appeal to people in Alabama as well as it can appeal to people in New York", said Dean recently. "We have gone from election to election, and, if we don't win, then we've dug ourselves into a deep hole and we have nothing to start with," he said and added, "That is a cycle that has to be broken." This has infuriated the Establishment Democrats, elected officials and large donors alike.

So, they are purposefully challenging Chairman Dean's leadership of the Party because they see him as the most high-ranking Progressive in the Party. With this challenge, they hope to maintain their spectacular record of losing (all branches of the Federal government, most State legislatures and Governor's offices as well). To emphasize his disdain for the Progressive Movement, Rahm Emanuel is going around the country handpicking unknowns and so-called moderates and then lavishing DCCC money and endorsements on them to defeat Progressive candidates in the primaries wherever he can. He says that we shouldn't rock the boat with the Republicans and then shows his true colors by attempting to quash any and all Progressive Democrats. Chuck Schumer is playing the same game. "When the far-left wing of the Democratic Party runs the Party, we lose," Mr. Schumer said at one fund-raiser.

If you believe in the Liberal Ideal, the Progressive Movement and demand a Democratic Party that is accountable to the membership first and not corporations, then join with the Progressive Caucus of the California Democratic Party in our action to support DNC Chair, Gov. Howard Dean and his 50 state strategy. Use the flyer attached and email, fax, phone and send a message of support to Chair Howard Dean that, "We've Got Your Back."

DNC Chairman
Gov. Howard Dean
"We've Got Your Back"

*We, the Progressive Majority of the Democratic Party, enthusiastically support our DNC Chair, Gov. Howard Dean, and his historic **"50 state plan"** to organize the party from the Grassroots up.*

I have proposed the following action and the flyer that accompanies it in order to oppose the DLC, Corporate Cronies and the Establishment Democrats attempt to thwart the Progressive movement. While Dean may not be our perfect leader, he is perceived by all of the above as one of our, if not the most, visible leaders. Whatever the truth of that is for us, it is a truth for them.

They have formed the "Data Warehouse" for Hill to run a divisive campaign ala the RAC-Rovians in our midst. They will target wedge issues to cleave the Liberals from the Progressives. It will be a campaign of fear.

They have formed the "Hamilton Project" at the Brookings Institute to cover their attack on Progressives, Liberals, the unions and the middle working class with that same old argument of "responsibility" masquerading as a front for "business is all", "money before members", "cash before citizens" and "pigs at the trough." It is designed to bolster their NAFTA/CAFTA loving capitulation to the forces of inequality so dear to Wall Street and K Street under the guise of, "Oh well, globalism is gonna hurt everybody." Not them, the incumbents and 1%ers.

While we proceed on all of our other agenda points, this is a not so subtle but difficult to attack slap on their pasty white faces. It will divert their energy and put them on the spot, off guard, while supporting the Party and pushing the so-called moderates over the side.

It started with the Wealthy Donors grousing about Dean's not listening to them and collecting most of the DNC $$$$$ from small donors. News flash, in the 2004 cycle, at least 40% of all $$$$ raised by both parties at all levels was from small donors. It is the future and the present and wrests control from their grubby sweaty palms.

I could go on but I think you get the point.

(Speech given at the CDP Progressive Caucus meeting April 2006)

DNC Chairman
Gov. Howard Dean
"We've Got Your Back"

We, the Progressive Majority of the Democratic Party, enthusiastically support our DNC Chair, Gov. Howard Dean, and his historic **"50 state plan"** to organize the party from the Grassroots up.

We, Progressive and Liberal Democrats, reject the failed leadership of the DLC, so-called Moderate Democrats and their Corporate allies whose 15 years of spectacular electoral failure have cost the Nation so dearly.

We strongly urge the DNC to pursue a policy of Progressive Action and Reform across America. Democrats must put an end to the era of capitulation to the Republican Anarchy Collective, its disastrous decade of Empire building abroad and narrow self-interests at home.

We, the people, reaffirm the original motto of the Republic of the United States of America, "E Pluribus Unum"!

NAME: _____

ADDRESS: _____

EMAIl: _____

Democratic National Committee
430 S. Capitol St. SE
Washington, DC 20003
PHONE: (202) 863-8000
FAX: (202) 863-8174
EMAIL: howarddean@dnc.org
www.democrats.org

(Flyer from the CDP Progressive Caucus meeting April 2006)

Framing the Movement Out of the Picture

June 2006

OK, I get it. Howard is not ideologically pure. But then again, who is? Erin Flynn is one of our best member/leaders and I enjoy any conversation we can have together about politics but her analysis of this action misses the side of this barn by a country mile or city block. This isn't a college lecture hall trying to figure out who said the right thing at the right time to the right person. Although both are necessary from time to time, waiting for Godot or wandering around Dublin in existential angst - this ain't. This is a real time struggle for the not only the soul of the Party but who has their hands on the steering wheel.

Let me ask you all the rock bottom question as I see it here: whom would you rather have as DNC Chair, Howard Dean or Chuck Schumer? Jane Harman or Marcy Winograd? Howard Dean may not be Marcy Winograd but Chuck Schumer is Jane Harman. This is a pivotal battle of the DLC Establishment Corporatists versus the nascent Progressive Liberal Movement. There is a real politik, right versus left, in this dogfight. Whether you like it or not, Howard Dean represents us in this process. Rahm Emanuel, Chuck Schumer, Al From, Hillary and Bill Clinton, James Carville and Paul Begala are actively seeking his defeat and removal from office. This is as plain as the look of bewilderment on Shrub's face.

Let's look at it in another way. When the forces of righteousness and indignation rose up in California, crashed the gate of the CDP and passed overwhelmingly the first Out of Iraq Resolution in the nation, who was watching and trying to defeat us? Art Torres? Howard Dean? Nancy Pelosi? Were we the inconvenient truth in the room? Yes, we were and remain so. Did all of the leaders have to acknowledge our truth and justice? Yes, they did. Power only accedes to a demand. Are the DLC hawks, Neo-Liberals and MobCorp expecting us to back Dean? No, they are surprised and possibly shocked. Are the Clintonistas correct in their assumption that the Governor Doctor is our putative leader? No, they are not. Do they have a clue as to who we are and what we want and what we are up to? They think they do but they do not. However, they have developed a tactic to drive us away from the center of Party infrastructure and power and it includes the elimination of Howard Dean as DNC Chair. Hey, it worked for them in the Presidential Election process, why not here and now?

It's time for us to realize, and I can't put too fine a point on this, that this Progressive Movement is now squarely up against the tight grasp for power being exerted by those whose lives it threatens to destroy. Oh come on Brad, it can't be that picturesque? Well, Dorothy, we are not in Kansas any longer. This is hardball on the street or any hackneyed metaphor you want to ascribe to it; this is war by other means. Did any of us think that they, the DLC jalopy of ambiguity, were just going to quietly walk away from their power, their pensions, their perks or their demographied, focused to death assumptions? Wake up people. We are the end of their road not just the beginning of ours. They have a lot to lose. We have a lot to gain. That means trouble with a capitol T, that rhymes with C and stands for Cash, cold hard Money.

All they have is money. All we have is the truth and the people. Who will prevail? Stick around and we shall see. In the meantime, they have chosen this battle over the Chair of the Party because of their fear of us. It's not what we would have chosen. Many of us assumed that these were fellow Democrats. Check it. The election that just passed right here in Southern California, showed us that the majority of incumbent Democrats from County Central Committee to State Central Committee to the State Legislature to the Congress are with the DLC. Why? Power baby - power and money. This is naked power and money at stake not idealism.

We cannot allow Dean to lose his control over the infrastructure of the Party as the Chair. You have to support anybody who can make Rahm Emanuel storm out of their office screaming expletives about how they don't understand that the DLC rules the party. You just have to. What a thing of beauty that must have been.

So I say again, support the Chair and his 50 state plan, no matter how lame you think it is and send a message to the Right-Wing DLC Power Poppin' Pusillanimous Pretenders that We the People Count, as Howard said in his call to action. Oh yeah, and you have to know he is getting our message by the way he signed off... Thank you for your leadership.

Veritas Est Vis
Brad Parker

CALIFORNIA BURNING:
The Struggle for Political Power in the California Democratic Party

April 2007

The flurry of interest, activity and excitement surrounding the January 2007 Assembly District elections in California was no accident. This once obscure intraparty election was hotly contested as a result of the long term organizing efforts of the Progressive Caucus of the CDP, laid out in their Progressive Plan, and by the Progressive Movement, inside and outside of the Party, in its many local, statewide and national manifestations. The Progressive Caucus itself though, is the result of a long simmering debate in the nation and the Democratic Party that has become a struggle for political power within the Party.

In order to better understand the game – as in game theory not idle entertainment – we need to know who the players are. However, there is no absolute dividing line between the opposing sides. In fact, we find some politicos playing both sides of the debate as it suits their personal ambitions. In the main though, there are two opposing sides, which can be defined by the ideas, issues and candidates, they support.

For most activists and hacks, the two factions vying for power are the Progressives and the DLC (Democratic Leadership Council). There are many identifying characteristics of both groups, which as we proposed, can be defined by the ideas and candidates they both embrace. Progressives, by in large, represent the left or Liberal wing of the Party and DLC members represent the right or Conservative wing of the Party. Bill & Hillary Clinton, Rahm Emanuel, Chuck Schumer, Joe Lieberman, Paul Begala, Terry McAuliffe and James Carville lead the DLC. Progressives, on the other hand, are led by their broad based self-identified "swarm" of citizen/activist members. Following swarm theory models - studied in science to explain the behavior of colonies of ants, flocks of birds or a school of fish - modern organizers, Progressives, tend toward membership consensus rather than top-down leadership edicts. This consensus is facilitated by person-to-person connections over the Internet and meet-ups on the ground. Just as the Internet is reorganizing every aspect of social and group interaction, it has radically altered political dynamics. So, there is no leader of the Progressive Movement, inside or outside of the Democratic Party but rather a visible, self aware and efficient, albeit chaotic – We The People.

Generally speaking, the DLC views itself as a pragmatic, winning is the only thing that counts, candidates are more important than ideas, traditional style political movement. Progressives view themselves as a principles first, people before profit, membership before leadership, modern, citizen-led political movement. Let's break it down even further:

- The DLC voted for the War in Iraq
- Progressives organized against the War in Iraq
- The DLC can't decide how to end the War
- Progressives say start leaving Iraq now
- The DLC supports better healthcare
- Progressives support single-payer universal healthcare
- The DLC believes incumbency is a right conferred
- Progressives believe that incumbency is a privilege earned
- The DLC believes in big money private donor election financing
- Progressives believe in public clean money election financing

These are a few among the many differences. In the area of Civil Rights, the DLC believes that the separation of church and state can be taken down and that narrow religious doctrine can be a guide to legislation. Progressives believe that our unalienable civil rights are not subject to the dogma of any religion, that no woman can be denied dominion over her own person and her reproductive rights and that every consenting adult may marry or join in a civil union with any other consenting adult.

These and other deep ideological differences culminate in the decisions made by the Party, at every level, on which candidates to support. Given that the DLC adherents have largely controlled the Party since 1988, it is no surprise that most candidates currently come from their ranks. But that is changing.

Belying their doctrine of winning is everything; the DLC eventually lost every body of the federal government, most statehouses and legislatures to the Republicans during the Clinton ascendancy. During the years of Republican dominance, the DLC found it pragmatic to capitulate to Republican cut and gut governance – NAFTA, the Telecommunications Act of 1996, the War in Iraq etc. - and thus arose the awakened citizen/activists. A dearth of ideas and the seduction of big money had hollowed out the DLC philosophy and effectiveness along with the Democratic Party. It was at this very point where California, like other states, caught on fire, the Progressive Movement fire. Now, California's fire is burning down the House of the old Democratic Party and it is spreading.

Let's examine the November 2006 elections.

Defining the fault line between the DLC and Progressives was the race for the senate in Connecticut. Ned Lamont soundly defeated Joe Lieberman in the Democratic primary. Jiltin' Joe decided to go with the Republicans, ran as a faux independent and beat Lamont in the general election. Republicans were not alone in supporting Joe. The silence of his DLC comrades in the House and Senate, confirmed their support as well. Joe was rewarded with important chairmanships of committees in the new Democratic Senate - just to show how grateful the

Party was that he had defeated the Progressive Democrat.

What about the new and bluer congress that was miraculously born as a result of the 2006 elections? Rahm Emanuel claims that the DLC handpicked candidates in the House led the way to the new majority. In fact, the truth is quite the opposite. Most of the new Democrats in the House are from the Progressive ranks.

In California and across the nation, the DCCC and the DSCC had searched for DLC candidates to run against Progressives in the primaries. They were more worried about the fire in the Party than the Republican opposition. They publicly attempted to orchestrate a victory that would give them more DLC and less Progressive members in the new Congress. In the end, they failed. The result in the House was more Progressives elected and joining the Progressive caucus to make it the largest caucus in the House. The Establishment DLC Democrats did succeed to some degree in the Senate. However, even the Senate was won by the expansive Progressive Liberal Democratic turnout and the Republican self-immolation.

The DLC and its leadership, led by the Clintons, Emanuel and Schumer, have proven to be no friend to the Progressive Democrats or Democrats in general. In fact, the DLC and its establishment cohorts in California are busily attempting to prevent the inevitable Progressive redesign of the Party.

First, all incumbent Democrats in the House, Progressive and DLC, secretly agreed that no incumbent Democrat would endorse any challenger in the 2006 primary. So, in a surreal twist, Blue Dog Democrats (a DLC caucus in the House), including California Reps. Ellen Tauscher and Jane Harman, found themselves endorsed by Progressive members of the House. This non-democratic and awkward agreement was crafted by the DLC leadership of the DCCC to thwart Progressive challengers.

Next, the establishment Democrats manipulated the tension between different unions – as well as their rank and file and leadership - to scuttle the Clean Money Proposition 89, at meetings of the CDP and during the general election in 2006. A palpable fear of true publicly financed campaigns grips the major donors of both parties and the consultants. For good measure, the CDP and some County Central Committees blithely failed to support Progressive candidates in many races for unstated reasons. Incumbency, endorsement and big money are arrogantly tightening their grip on power in a vain attempt to hold back the changing of the guard. However, all during the primaries and the general election, the Progressive Caucus of the California Democratic Party was organizing for another election.

Part two of the Progressive Plan, put forward by the caucus in the summer of 2006, called upon all Progressives inside and outside of the Party to join together and get elected to more of the voting seats inside the Party. Together with PDA and DFA, the CDP Progressive Caucus used its micro-media network – email, e-newsletters and e-action alerts – to great effect and the Progressive swarm showed its rising strength in this January's AD Elections. Progressives won a majority of the 960 delegate seats to the DSCC – Democratic State Central Committee - and an increasing number of the 80 delegate seats to the Executive Board. This will surely change the nature of the votes taken by these two bodies in the next two years. That in turn will challenge the DLC dominance of the Party.

Next on the horizon is the CDP 2007 Convention in San Diego. There the debate will once again be joined with important votes on Party procedures for posting the names of all voting members of the DSCC and its Executive Board on the CDP website and moving the election of the DNC members from the 300 person Executive Board to the 3000 member DSCC.

The rise of the Progressive Movement inside the Democratic Party was inevitable. Technology does not take a vote on its effects, they just happen. The Internet is turning the Pyramid of Power upside down throughout every aspect of society across the globe. Those who survive and thrive will adapt to its architecture, which is creating a new horizontal power structure. Those who attempt to control its effects will be swept away along with the antiquated top-down structures that have dominated human social evolution. Local, sustainable, renewable and humane systems are on the verge of sweeping the planet thanks to the Internet and the ever-widening Age of Information. The struggle for power in the

California Democratic Party is only one of the myriad examples of the impact of this new technology and its embrace by citizens far and wide.

In fairness, we must assert that all of the participants in this epic struggle for power in the Democratic Party are citizens who believe that their strategies and tactics for claiming and holding political power are in the best interests of the nation. And it must be said that even when the ideological divide between the two main factions of the Party has become rancorous and divisive, this power struggle is more a debate than a war. This debate has produced great enmity from time to time on both sides. Enmity has escalated to nasty political tactics and various low-end shenanigans in some cases. But the contentious dialogue and electoral wrangling has produced more light than heat and will in the end create a truly Progressive Liberal Democratic Party. Ignited by the fire of the Progressive Movement, the California Democratic Party is burning, down to ashes. Then like the proverbial phoenix, a new Party will arise. The same will be true of the national Democratic Party.

California is burning and sparks are gonna fly from this Wild West brush fire, so be prepared. Oh - and will the last person to leave the DLC please turn out the lights.

Martin's Way...

April 2007

As we head to the California Democratic Party convention in San Diego we find ourselves, Progressives and Liberals, in a crisis. At question is how do we confront our apparent enemies, the established old guard of the Democratic Party, most vividly embodied by the corporately controlled DLC, while maintaining our principles? We have a choice to make as to tactics: we can be enraged or engaged. The Chinese pictograph for crisis contains two elements: chaos and opportunity. While we struggle with the leadership for the soul of the Party we must ask ourselves if the chaos of stoking the fire of rage will get us to our goal or will the vigorous engagement of debate and organizing present us with the opportunity to be more effective and long-lasting? Dr. Martin Luther King Jr., has served as our guide in this very crisis for many years. I think we should revisit his thoughts again today and remind ourselves of Martin's way.

Martin preached that, *"Non-cooperation and nonviolent resistance were means of stirring and awakening moral truths in one's opponents, of evoking the humanity which, Martin believed, existed in each of us. The means therefore had to consistent with the ends. And the end, as Martin conceived it, was greater than any of its parts, greater than any one single issue. ' The end is redemption and reconciliation', he believed. 'The aftermath of nonviolence is the creation of the*

Beloved Community, while the aftermath of violence is tragic bitterness.'"

That text is from the foreword to Martin's book, "Strength to Love." The book was written in 1963. Coretta Scott King wrote an introduction to the new edition in 1981 from which this quote was taken. "Strength to Love," is a collection of sermons that Martin delivered during the Montgomery Bus Boycott. The crisis of that time and the actions that were debated mirror our times and our debate on what path to take today. Martin and Coretta may not be with us today on the temporal plane but their spirit abides as a guide to our soul-searching. It is in that spirit that we may find the way forward.

On the one hand, we might opt for the emotional release of disruptive theater planned to humiliate the leadership and the electeds. We could be aggressive and get in their face. We could act out even to the point of destruction of property and physical violence. Or, we could just stand up in every meeting where they gather and shout them down. While this may feel righteous at the moment, it will be followed by a let down and then depression when all it garners is fleeting attention and renewed resistance from those whose policies we oppose. This is always the case with aggressive and violent behavior; just imagine the aftermath of our withdrawal from Iraq or reflect on Vietnam.

On the other hand, we could choose the long hard road of steadfast engagement, debate and organizing. We could become the Party infrastructure by organizing to get elected at every level and in every body of the Party, thus becoming the voting majority on the inside of the Democratic Party, not just outside. We could challenge our opponents to public debate on the issues. If they won't debate then we can propose the ideas to move America forward and present them at every political forum, large and small, public and private. We can engage the public, the Party and our opposition on "policy" not personality," in person and on the Internet and thereby lead the discussion and the action in the political arena, as we already are.

Through continued participation at every level of the process, the promotion of principled positions and unrelenting demands for accountability, we can awaken the soul of the Democratic Party. When we have transformed the Democratic Party and restored the Liberal Ideal to the core of the Party's actions, we can send thousands of Progressive Liberals into office and make our policy the law of the land. With the diligence we must demand of ourselves, we can demand the same from our government.

If we propose to be the new leadership of the Democratic Party and America, then we must let go of the Republican induced politics of violent personality destruction. We must present ourselves as the principled nonviolent strength of ideas and the tenacity and tough-mindedness to put them into practice. We must not only know what we are against but what we are for and we must stay true to our path of peace. Not just peace instead of war between nations but peace among ourselves.

When the civil war ended, Lincoln chose the song, "Dixie," to be played at his second inaugural, where he solemnly remarked, "...with malice toward none, with charity for all..." We should do the same. We should resist the temptation in ourselves to become what we behold in our opponents. Instead we should fulfill the promise we made to ourselves decades ago to live by, with and for peace, love and understanding. Stay engaged not enraged. Keep the peace. Create the Beloved Community. It's Martin's way. Let it be our guide.

A Weekend at the Circus
(Swarming the beach at CDP/San Diego)

May 2007

Once upon a time there was a clown named Crony. Crony the clown was obscenely wealthy and had very particular special interests. Crony decided that he wanted to buy the circus. Not content to merely watch the performers, Crony decided to ride the Elephant. While Crony was riding the pachyderm it went insane and started to trample the crowd. This was embarrassing for Crony so he switched to riding the Donkey. In a short while the Donkey became a Jackass. And this dear reader is where we find ourselves today.

Now that the Crony Corporatists have ridden the Republicans into the ground and saddled the Democrats with the DLC leadership, every branch of the government is imploding into tepid ineffectiveness, grim graft and corpulent corruption. Major donor campaign contributions have oozed over the political landscape, creating a sludge of legal bribery that has brought our fledgling democracy to its knees. But Mother Nature, ever mindful of preserving balance in all her domain, has given birth to a movement to counteract this imparity, the Progressive Movement.

How will it work? Take the example of Global Warming. Either humans switch from the use of extractables – coal, oil, natural gas and uranium – or the emissions and waste from their use for energy will eliminate humanity and balance will be restored. As it is in this example, so it will be in matters of state and policy, which brings us to the latest chapter of the struggle for the soul of the Democratic Party that occurred this year at the California Democratic Party convention in San Diego.

Debate is anathema to the DLC, Blue Dogs, Establishment Democrats and their courtiers, the lobbyists and consultants. Why? They won't debate because they can't win a debate of ideas; they have none. All they posses are their discredited neo-liberal rationales, spewed forth from the dubiously monikered Progressive Policy Institute, the Third Way and the Democratic Leadership Council – the DLC. The smoke and mirrors promulgated by these Clinton-led men behind the curtain fronts are thinly veiled propaganda broadsides for the Cronies. In our current parlance, they are nothing more than political "greenwashing." Greenwashing is defined as: the dissemination of misleading information by an organization to conceal its abuse of the environment in order to present a positive public image. In this case, it's the political environment.

So, the DLC establishment, too craven to debate, has given up that field of struggle due to their paucity of ideas and stupendous flops at the polls. They have now retreated to parliamentary procedure and Roberts Rules of Order to stabilize their waning control over the Party. That tactic was on full display in San Diego at the CDP convention.

With great irony, the conservative wing of the Party did everything they could, including bad faith bargaining at the last minute, to preserve the resolution they most coveted, the so-called 'Unity in 08" resolution and to stifle debate on the truly important issues of the day, transparency, accountability and open access to information, not to mention race, economics and war – Dr. King's triple evils. All weekend, the will of the majority of delegates and Democrats across the state was squashed by referrals, arcane rules and a quorum call in the name of pragmatism, Presidential candidates and "Unity." The only question that remained after our weekend at the circus was; who orchestrated this obfuscation?

Have no fear dear reader. In the end, it doesn't matter who did what. This was not a setback for the forces of nature – the Progressive Movement – it was a revelation. Some of the leadership is for the membership and some are only in it for their career. Some are desperately asserting their primacy in all matters politic and others are with us and relieved that we finally showed up. Everything is proceeding according to the Progressive Plan.

There are now three rings in our Party Circus. On the right, are the DLC Establishment Democrats led by Crony the Clown and the Clinton coterie. On the left, is the majority of the membership of the Party - and now a growing number of the leadership - led by no leader save our own conscience. In the middle, are the majority of the leadership and a minority of the membership led by fear-induced pragmatism generated by focus groups, polls and Crony the Clown. The right ring is shrinking. The middle ring is experiencing defections to the left and the left ring is where the action is.

The establishment disarray, exemplified by the collapse of trust and order on Sunday April 29th in San Diego, signaled the end for the DLC twenty-year reign of shuck and jive, three card Monte, winning is everything Democrats. They are even more aware of this than Progressives are. For twenty years they led the Party down the yellow brick – i.e. Crony contributions – road to electoral insignificance. Only when the Progressives showed up in force in 2006 and the Republican meltdown was in full effect, did the Democratic Party make a comeback. So, the only question is what field of struggle will the DLC retreat to now, since they know we will prevail in the parliamentary procedure wrangle as well?

The last bastion for Crony and the DLC will be, no surprise here - money, large money and all its strings. Campaign contributions have devolved into legal bribery. If you want to win an election you have to get the big bucks pal. If you want the big bucks then you have to toe the Crony line. There are no exceptions, other than the occasional give the little people a crumb act in the center ring. Well, nature has provided a solution for this imbalance as well, Clean Money - full public campaign financing - and Net Neutrality.

Crony is thinking ahead too though and is busily going about hoodwinking Democrats into privatizing the Internet – Internet 2. If Crony can control the Internet – the future of worldwide communications and information – even without campaign cash, Crony can mold public opinion to his bidding. Sixty percent of all the websites in the world are political speech. They will be the first to go if Crony gobbles up the Internet. Union organizing sites and free speech of every kind will soon follow. Crony knows that Clean Money and Net Neutrality – the Internet as a public infrastructure, ala the Interstate Highway System not a toll road – will send Crony back to the boardroom and eventually into oblivion. Keep your eyes on the prize my friends not the dog and pony show.

Well, all in all it was quite a weekend as Progressives swarmed the beach in San Diego. The DLC was on the high wire with no net, while the Progressives were redesigning the tent, the rings and the midway. Thanks to PDA and the Progressive Caucus, Impeachment was back on the table and evolution was in the air. Roberts Rules brought anything but order to the proceedings and democracy threatened to break out at any moment. Maybe this donkey turned jackass has some kick left in it after all.

Oh, and one last thought: We, the people, love the inherent entertainment value of Party politics as much as anyone but are not amused by the 19th century style of whoever has the gold makes the rules. No one is showing up for that tired old act anymore unless you're a Republican. Democratic Party registration is going down for just that reason - the Crony rules. The only growing number of active delegates or registering members in our Party self identify as "Progressive." If anyone believes that we will be part of the same old circus with a new bunch of clowns they are mistaken.

Word to Crony: trade in your stock options and head for retirement or the next clown outfit you'll be wearing will be an orange jumpsuit or perhaps a smart black and white stripes ensemble. The circus is over. Let the Party begin!

Net Neutrality Resolution

July 2007

Democrats,

On July 15th 2007, the Executive Board of the California Democratic Party passed the following resolution in favor of Net Neutrality and affordable high speed Internet for America.

The adoption of this resolution was made possible by the unprecedented cooperation of both the Labor Caucus and the Progressive Caucus of the CDP. Working together over the months following the CDP convention in San Diego, representatives of both caucuses, led by Jim Gordon, chair of the Labor Caucus and Brad Parker, officer of the Progressive Caucus, were able to craft a resolution that addressed the concerns of both groups and Americans as a whole. Once again, after 100 years of organizing and political activism, Progressives and Union members have found common cause. Our hope is that this resolution will become a blueprint for legislation across the country that preserves Internet integrity with open, equal and impartial access and Net Neutrality. Further, that the build out of high speed Internet be undertaken as a public utility maintained by union members bringing affordable broadband Internet access to all Americans.

No issue of public governance is more critical at this time in our history than the immediate need for every level of government to pass and enforce legislation to embody the principles of this resolution. Therefore, we call upon every Democrat in America to send this resolution to every elected official across the nation and to insist that Net Neutrality and affordable high speed Internet become the law of the land.

Support of Affordable High Speed Internet for America And Internet Neutrality

WHEREAS to secure the rights of assembly, and free speech online, which are guaranteed by the Constitution and encourage new innovative American businesses to flourish, Americans are entitled to and require, open, equal and impartial Internet access; we need high speed internet for our homes, schools, hospitals and workplaces to grow jobs and our economy; enable innovations in telemedicine, education, public safety and government services; foster independence for people with disabilities and strengthen democratic discourse and civic participation and;

WHEREAS the United States - the country that invented the Internet - has fallen from first to sixteenth in internet adoption; US consumers pay more for slower speeds than people in other advanced nations; millions of Americans, especially in rural and low income areas do not have access to affordable, high speed broadband; the United States alone among the advanced nations has no national, Internet policy; the US definition of "high speed" at 200 kilobits per second (kbps) is too slow and has not changed in nine years: the US and California collection of broadband data does not tell us what we need to know about broadband deployment, adoption, speeds and prices and consumer and worker protections must be safeguarded on high speed networks and;

WHEREAS the growth of a free and open Internet has provided historic advances in the realms of democracy, free speech, communication, research and economic development; California and US consumers are entitled to and require open, unfettered access to the lawful Internet content of their choice without interference by any entity, public or private; build out of universal, high speed, high capacity networks will promote an open Internet by eliminating bandwidth scarcity;

THEREFORE BE IT RESOLVED that the California Democratic Party endorses national, state and local policies to promote affordable, high speed broadband for all with strong protections for consumers and the workers who build, maintain and service those networks; and a national goal for universal access and deployment of networks capable of delivering 10 megabits per second downstream and 1 megabit per second upstream by the year 2010 and the California Democratic Party supports federal and state initiatives to improve data collection on high speed broadband deployment, adoption, speed and prices as a necessary first step; upgrading the current definition of high speed to 2 megabits per second downstream, 1 megabit per second upstream and policies that promote public programs to stimulate build out of high speed networks to all homes and businesses in the nation and;

BE IT FURTHER RESOLVED that the California Democratic Party in order to promote vigorous free speech, a vibrant business community, and unfettered access to all information on the Internet, supports policies to preserve an open, neutral and interconnected Internet; protect against any degradation or blocking of access to any websites or content on the Internet and insure consumers have the right to free email; encourages build out of high speed networks to all homes and businesses so that everyone can go where they want and upload or download what they want on the Internet as a public utility maintained by union workers.

Submitted July 14th, 2007 by the
Labor Caucus of the California Democratic Party represented by Jim Gordon - Chair
Progressive Caucus of the California Democratic Party represented by Brad Parker – Officer

Adopted July 15th, 2007 by the
Executive Board of the California Democratic Party meeting in Sacramento, California.

Our Progressive Coalition
A Reason To Believe

November 2007

When we were formulating our strategy timeline for the "Progressive Plan" – published by the Progressive Caucus of the California Democratic Party in August 2006 – we called for a coalition meeting of all outside the Democratic Party Progressive groups with all Progressive Caucuses inside the state Democratic Parties in the fall of 2007. Up until two weeks ago, it looked as though this strategic prognostication might not be realized as the rest of the timeline has been. As we prepare to celebrate Thanksgiving, we can be thankful that in two significant ways this call to coalition has not only been realized but in mysterious and stimulating ways.

First – a move to censure Senator Dianne Feinstein for her votes to confirm Leslie Southwick and Michael Mukasey, that began in the Executive Board of the Progressive Caucus of the CDP, caught fire across California, resulting in a spirited effort to do just that at the CDP Executive Board meeting in Anaheim this past weekend. Mal Burnstein – Co-Chair of the Progressive Caucus of the CDP - first brought the resolution of censure to the caucus board. It was unanimously passed.

Then, it began to be moved and passed at Democratic Clubs and County Central Committees. That was concurrent with an all-out and energetic promotion by the Courage

Campaign. Before long the censure movement was joined by MoveOn, PDA, local DFA and Wellstone chapters and more than 30,000 Californians. Even though the Resolutions committee of the CDP voted to stifle debate and not hear the resolution - the Progressive, Women's and Irish-American caucuses passed it. California was on fire again.

Less heralded - but just as important - was the announcement of an Immigration Town Hall to be held at the 2008 CDP Convention in San Jose this March. This initiative also originated in the Progressive Caucus Executive Board. Over the last six months, the Labor caucus embraced it, as did the Women's and African-American caucuses, finally receiving the imprimatur of CDP Chairman Art Torres at this weekend's CDP meetings. It is a bold idea to bring together representatives of all of the caucuses in the Party who choose to participate and discuss an issue central to the upcoming 2008 campaigns in a setting that encourages listening, dialogue and mutual respect. A coalition of seemingly disparate groups within the Party forming a consensus is also a feature of the "Progressive Plan" strategic timeline and was slated for the 2008 CDP Convention, where it will now come to fruition. Where the members lead, the leaders must follow.

Bound up in the drama surrounding these policy and action determinations has been the question – "Who is a Democrat?" and "What does the Democratic Party stand for?" While there are as many answers as there are registered Democrats, both questions taken together point toward a larger phenomena that we are all participating in – futuring the Democratic Party.

Broadly speaking, there are two forces that might be categorized as: the progressive membership (inside and outside of the Party – the activists) and the current leadership (both Party leaders and elected officials) who are debating these questions and pointing to their divergent philosophies for answers. Current leadership seems to be embattled and demanding unity behind incumbents and campaigns as well as established Party funding, endorsement, rules, resolutions and platform procedures. Progressive membership is rallying for more openness, access to decision-making apparatus, accountability of electeds (and their voting records), transparency in financial decisions, disbursement of campaign funds to all candidates and open debate of all issues. It may appear that these two camps are antithetical but that is not necessarily so.

Current leadership claims that critique of Democrats by Democrats leads to Republican victories. Progressive membership counters that lack of critique by Democrats of both Democrats and Republicans leads to inertia, capitulation and complicity in Republican malfeasance. So, what can bring the apparently opposed views into consilience? How can the Democratic Party develop improved strategies for advancing the Liberal Ideal? What is the best way to bring about an end to Neo-Con social policy and Neo-Liberal economic policy? When do Democrats do best at winning elections? The answer is simple and profound; give the citizens of America a "reason to believe."

In a nation mired in scandal – political, business and religious – people have lost hope. When Party leaders are incommunicado from the citizenry. When elected officials are enjoying fine wine, luxury travel, substantial healthcare and pension plans yet the citizens have none. When politicians tell you to trust them and yet they betray their own families – in public. When the first consideration on any vote is how will it help an elected to get reelected. When too many people are dying for no reason in an illegal war of intervention in a foreign land. When there's too much cash from Crony contributions spilling out of the campaign accounts of electeds and the working stiffs have nothing then the people become mired in despair and the Constitution gathers dust in a forgotten corner. Our job as Progressives is now, has always been and will remain to give people a reason to believe again.

While we are dispatching the Republican Anarchy Collective – and we are getting there – we must take on the Crony corruption in the Democratic Party. The source of the corruption – besides primal greed and narrow self-interest – is the theoretical premise foisted upon our Party by the DLC. Their premise was and is; money and business are the primary concerns of the Party along with aggressive national security. Of course, this thesis was always false but with a salesman like Bill Clinton the Party couldn't resist. Now, twenty years of devastating electoral losses later the membership has woken up and begun to swarm around the Progressive movement. In the end, money was not the way to win but the way to lose. Even the current leadership and electeds are beginning to tire of carrying the Clinton/DLC machine around on their backs.

So, our job as a Progressive coalition remains the same. We are here to give the people, the sullen citizens, a reason to believe; a reason to believe that their vote will be counted as cast, a reason to believe that the Liberal Ideal is not dead, a reason to believe that principles win elections not big donors, a reason to believe that they should be active civically, a reason to believe that the Democratic Party is different from the Republican Party, a reason to register as Democrats and vote for Democrats. In short – the Progressive membership's emphasis on principles is the cure for what ails the body politic. Our forming swarming coalition is the reason to believe.

This past weekend showed that everyone, members, leaders, activists and electeds alike could and should find a way to work together for the enlightened self-interests of all. It put a fine note on the reality that only the freedom of "dissent" can lead to the "consent" of the governed. It also proved that accountability and standing for something is not only possible but also essential to being a Democrat and the future of the Democratic Party. Most importantly, the Progressives inside the Party acted with decorum and civility – allowing the strength of our ideas and our tough-mindedness to carry our message, while many in the opposition lost their cool and relied on bellicose belligerence to defend their derisory obfuscation. Our principled ideas and actions are our strength and speak louder for us than emotional outbursts ever will.

If Democrats want to win again - then they only need to stand up, show up and speak up for the principles we all hold dear rather than the large donor's pet projects. Our Progressive Coalition not only stands for all Americans but is the positive force forging a reason to believe while creating - E Pluribus Unum. To paraphrase Hubert Horatio Humphrey – I'm as pleased as punch to be part of this historic citizens movement of the Twenty First Century. I can't wait for another wild weekend!

Control or Facilitation?
The Immigration Town Hall
At the 2008 CDP Convention

May 2008

Progressives had many things to feel good about during the 2008 CDP Convention in San Jose. There were some long sought gains made for principles and the people - especially on the Platform Committee and our new, mostly Progressive platform. However, the fate of the Immigration Town Hall, initiated by the Progressive Caucus, was a donkey of another color.

On the positive side: for the first time a broad spectrum of caucuses collaborated on an important and controversial issue. Together, nine caucuses presented their consensus positions at an open to the DSCC delegates Town Hall, during a general session. This was followed by a brief amount of comment from the floor by the delegates. That's the good stuff. Following are the curious shortcomings of the event.

When the concept was first put forward, it was designed to open up the dialogue surrounding a critical issue - get ahead of the Republicans for the general election. It was conceived from the experience the Progressive Caucus had derived by holding several Town Halls. Our feeling was that there was too much talking from the podium and not enough listening to the members on the floor. Next, we wanted to include several other caucuses for outreach. We organized with the Labor, Women's, African-American and Chicano-Latino caucuses and when we asked for a room to present this event, at the November CDP E. Bd., the current CDP leadership said they wanted to be involved. So, we met to lay out the concept and form an organizing committee.

At that meeting, in November, we came to a basic agreement on the meeting outline - as a Town Hall with as much member comment time as possible. We insisted that interaction was the key - not a lecture. It was agreed that we have just a little background and a statistical speaker, followed by caucus representatives and then the bulk of the time for member's comments. In addition, all of the CDP caucuses would be invited to participate. That was the intent. The effect was remarkably different.

Instead of a separate meeting the event was folded into a general session. Then, things really began to unravel. Time allotted for speakers, chosen only by the CDP leadership with no input from the caucuses, grew. Time for the critical input from caucus speakers shrank. Membership time sank like the Titanic. When the event happened on Saturday - it was apparent that the original idea of inclusion had been dropped in favor of more of the usual talking heads. We were marginalized.

First - we had to follow the seemingly endless list of electeds and candidates that ate up all of the morning session time. After that wore everyone out, the ITH began one and a half hours late and at the end of the morning general session, as everyone was leaving to attend the lunch. The selected speakers ate up 30 minutes of time after some important and cogent remarks by Congressmember Zoe Lofgren. As the clocked ticked - more delegates vacated the premises. Next, each of the nine participating caucuses - Labor, Chicano-Latino, African-American, Business and Professional, Irish-American, Rural, Asian/Pacific Islander, Senior and Progressive - gave very brief 90 second remarks. You could hear the crickets. This was followed by a handful of questions, hilariously dominated by LaRouche devotees who had stacked the mikes. By the time the closing remarks came - the hall was essentially empty.

Not only were there hardly any delegates in the hall for the Town Hall but also the staging was awkward. The speakers panel sat on the dais while the caucus representatives had to deliver their remarks from a microphone on a lower level with dim lighting. It looked like the kids table at a Thanksgiving dinner. To add insult to injury; the event was never publicized in an email to the delegates, on the CDP website or on the printed agenda of the general session. Only a paltry flyer with little information was handed out on the day of the meeting and in too few places to create a buzz.

You might assume that this was an exercise in futility dear reader but you would be wrong. It was an exercise in discovery.

All of the caucuses organized in good faith and found that they can work together on important issues. That will resonate positively through the membership for some time to come.

On the other hand - the current CDP leadership by their actions and not their intent showed that they are lost in the old paradigm of control rather than moving into the 21st century paradigm of facilitation - powered by the Internet. By marginalizing this event, attempting to hide it from the delegates and the public, while pretending to be cooperating, they gave a bold demonstration of their true state of mind - Vis a Vis - this type of event, the membership and the caucuses. We all know that what's important in relationships is not what you say but what you do.

We can and must accept that the actions of the leadership came from good intentions but their effect was the opposite. One is left to wonder if it was contempt, fear or dismissiveness that produced this sad scene of a great idea mangled in public. Here was an opportunity for the current leadership of the CDP to embrace inclusion and bold initiative but it was lost. Oh well - on to our next innovation in the democratization of information and consensus igniting action.

So, here's to the lessons learned and now, let us press onward with the membership, as ably represented by the caucuses, dedicated to openness, transparency and accountability.

We will do this again, as a product of collaboration among the caucuses. Next time the effect will exemplify the intent and courage will outweigh fear. Next time the event will reflect and not direct the membership. See you there.

LEAVING HOME

June 2008

My report is on the Progressive Plan.

Sisters and brothers - the only milestone on the Strategic timeline found on page 9 of the Progressive Plan that we failed to meet was the call for a Progressive Coalition to be formed of inside and outside the Party Progressive groups in the fall of 2007.

I believe that this DNC Election has revealed the reason why. Leaving home is hard to do... but leaving the comfort of home is the only way to go further...

Our advancement inside the Party in the last four years has brought the Progressive movement to the brink of a broader leadership role. The question is - how will we evolve to claim that leadership role and show the way forward for the Party?

Some members of the Progressive Swarm favor defeating Democrats and Republicans who vote against the interests of the people and in favor of Crony business, politics and government. That is an undeniable necessity. Some Progressives favor electing more Progressive Democrats to carry our policy and craft it into law. That is an essential imperative. Others have been working inside the Party to establish a Progressive infrastructure that can be maintained and handed down. That is the crux of the Progressive Plan.

What we have discovered in our vigorous efforts to accomplish the first two tasks is that the unfinished business of the third task has proven to be the lynchpin in the establishment's defense of incumbency, endorsement and big money donors. We have chipped away at it and even had some marginal success. However, significant transformative change is just beyond our grasp within the Party processes, where entrenched interests are capable of out-voting us on the floor of most bodies of the Party.

How then, can we come up with the necessary "change" votes when we have at most 30% to 40% of the votes in any one body? The only available answer is - outreach and coalition with other courageous souls within each body of the Party. We don't have the luxury of time to go through cycle after cycle of elections to gain more members, while the world crumbles around us. In other words - we must allow our movement to evolve.

If we hold 35% to 40% of the votes, as we do, on any important issue that comes before the DSCC or its Executive Board, then we need 16% to 11% of the remaining votes to prevail on an issue - 50% plus one.

So, how do we become the faction of the Party that realigns the vote and becomes the new leadership? Inclusion.

Our task at this point in time, as we foresaw it in the 2006 Progressive Plan, is to reach out to the Liberals and through collaboration, dialogue and rigorous debate, get them to invest in our Progressive Policy:

"We must join with our natural allies, Liberal Democrats, and even though we may know many Democrats who are right wing or cooperating with Republicans and Establishment power brokers we must remain inclusive and welcome them back to their principles as well. As we sweep the DLC cabal from the Democratic Party we should leave open the possibility of growth for every Democrat. Our Progressive Plan begins in California, proceeds to every state in the union, and culminates in a Progressive Democratic National Committee." That's from Page 6 of the Plan signed by all of the officers of this board and ratified by the membership.

In order to accomplish that, both sides must overcome their inherent fear of the other. Liberals fear our policy because they are uncomfortable with the pace and scope of change that we prescribe. Progressives fear that any coalition will weaken our policy. Neither fear is necessary. As the infamous blues singer Robert Johnson once wailed, "I went down to the crossroads." We are at the crossroads now.

It is up to us, Progressives, to show the way forward. Courage overcomes fear. That is leadership. That is our destiny and destiny beckons.

We need to find liberals that will work on our policy with us, one issue at a time, and build mutual trust. Then we must take the time to explain why Progressive policy is the cure for what ails the body politic. We must instill in our new partners the reality that there is no time to waste on these vital issues. We need to convince them that gradualism is an untenable model for change:

"This is no time to engage in the luxury of cooling off or to take the tranquilizing drug of gradualism. Now is the time to make real the promises of democracy." - That's from Dr. Martin Luther King Jr.'s, "I Have a Dream" speech.

When we go beyond our comfort zone and bring the light of tolerance, understanding and inclusion to as many as we can, then we will have fulfilled our promise to each other to be different than the practices of exclusion, derision, mistrust and dismissiveness that we beheld when we came together in the Party. We are the change and anyone should be able to join us in that change. And we should be able to join with them, bound by Progressive policy.

This coming election of a new CDP - DNC delegation is an opportunity for both Progressives and Liberals to begin the realignment and form a coalition that will move the Party into the 21st Century. This election is a possible pivot away from fear and toward cooperation. Let us approach every corner of the Democratic Party with our Progressive Principles and Policy in one hand and with the other hand open to welcome others into a new understanding, a new and better inclusion. To paraphrase John Lennon - you say you want an evolution? Then let us go out to the Party, the nation and the world and grow one.

Let's go further...
Vote for a Progressive DNC !!!
Don't Breakdown... Breakthrough !!!

E PLURIBUS UNUM
you say you want an evolution…

June 2008

Three small words and one very BIG idea: E Pluribus Unum - "out of many, one." It is easy to say but troublesome to achieve. Our advancement inside the Party in the last four years has brought the Progressive movement to the brink of a broader leadership role. The question is - how will we evolve to claim that leadership role and show the way forward for the Democratic Party? Even more vexing is: will we be able to stand together to lead or will the pressure of the task - turning the ship of state back to the left and the forces of the status quo - prove overwhelming?

Some members of the Progressive Swarm favor defeating Democrats and Republicans who vote against the interests of the people and in favor of Crony business, politics and government. That is an undeniable necessity. Some Progressives favor electing more Progressive Democrats to carry our policy and craft it into law. That is a formidable task but an essential imperative. Others have been working inside the Party to establish a Progressive infrastructure that can be maintained and handed down to succeeding generations. That is the crux of the Progressive Plan.

What we have discovered in our vigorous efforts to accomplish the first two tasks is that the unfinished business of the third task has proven to be the lynchpin in the establishment's defense of the bulwark of incumbency, endorsement and big money donors, which maintains the rightward drift of the body politic. We have chipped away at it and even had some marginal success. However, significant transformative change is just beyond our grasp within the Party processes, where entrenched interests are capable of out-voting us on the floor of most bodies of the Party.

How then, can we come up with the necessary "change" votes when we have at most 30% to 40% of the votes in any one body? We don't have the luxury of time to go through cycle after cycle of elections to gain more members, which we will do in any case, while the world crumbles around us. The only available answer is - outreach and coalition with Liberals and other courageous souls within each body of the Party. In other words - we must allow our movement to evolve.

If we hold 35% to 40% of the votes, as we do, on any important issue that comes before the DSCC or its Executive Board, then we need 16% to 11% of the remaining votes to prevail on an issue - 50% plus one. Where would those votes come from? They would naturally come from the Liberals.

As we posited in the Progressive Plan - Liberals are now the center of the Party. Moderates or Conservatives are on the Right of the Party. If Moderates hold 33% of the votes in any one body of the Party - local, state and national - and we believe that they do, then the third in the middle, Liberals, are the balance of power. So, how do we become the faction of the Party that realigns the vote and becomes the new leadership? Inclusion.

Our task at this point in time, as we foresaw it in the 2006 Progressive Plan, is to reach out to the Liberals and through collaboration, dialogue and rigorous debate, get them to invest in our Progressive Policy. In order to accomplish that, both sides must overcome their inherent fear of the other. Liberals fear our policy because they are uncomfortable with the pace and scope of change that we prescribe on a host of issues. Progressives fear that any coalition will weaken our policy.

As the infamous blues singer Robert Johnson once wailed, "I went down to the crossroads." Progressives fear that a Faustian bargain will be struck at the crossroads, where some members will sell their soul for personal advancement and water down Progressive policy in exchange for an elected or Party job. Liberals, down at the crossroads, fear that Progressives are the mythic left of old (that was actually just a ginned up scapegoat of the rabid right in a vain attempt to hold back the future - i.e. the Culture Wars) and will seduce them into straying from Main Street American values. Neither fear is necessary. It is up to us, Progressives, to show the way forward. Courage overcomes fear. That is leadership. That is our destiny and destiny beckons.

We need to find liberals that will work on our policy with us, one issue at a time, and build mutual trust. Then we must take the time to explain why Progressive policy is the cure for what ails the body politic. We must instill in our new partners the reality that there is no time to waste on these vital issues. We need to convince them that gradualism, as Dr. Martin Luther King Jr. taught us, is an untenable model for change:

"This is no time to engage in the luxury of cooling off or to take the tranquilizing drug of gradualism. Now is the time to make real the promises of democracy." - Dr. Martin Luther King Jr.'s, "I Have a Dream" speech, delivered August 28, 1963 at the Lincoln Memorial in Washington DC.

When we go beyond our comfort zone and bring the light of tolerance, understanding and inclusion to as many as we can, then we will have fulfilled our promise to each other to be different than the practices of exclusion, derision, mistrust and dismissiveness that we beheld when we came together in the Party. We are the change and anyone should be able to join us in that change. And we should be able to join with them, bound by Progressive policy.

This coming election of a new CDP - DNC delegation is an opportunity for both Progressives and Liberals to begin the realignment and form a coalition that will move the Party into the 21st Century. This election is a possible pivot away from fear and toward cooperation. Let us approach every corner of the Democratic Party with our Progressive Principles and Policy in one hand and with the other hand open to welcome others into a new understanding, a new and better inclusion.

To paraphrase John Lennon - you say you want an evolution? Then let us go out to the Party, the nation and the world and grow one.

All together now... E Pluribus Unum... further...

We are the People...

Part III

Stand Up, Show Up & Speak Up

I Am Opposed
(Speech delivered at the CDP convention - April 2005)

May 2005

I rise in opposition to

This unlawful and immoral WAR and those who profit from it

Religious intolerance that has
    condemned civil society and now threatens
    to extinguish the constitution

Corporate greed that breeds a wasteland of hate
    giving   birth to more hopeless lives of rage
    and oppression here and around the world

Rigged elections and soul less politicians on the
    take

Corruption at every level of American business
    and governance

I am opposed most of all to

Despair that leads to apathy and the indifference
    of people who know better, have much and
    proudly refuse to vote

I rise in support of

Clean Money Campaign Financing and election
    Protection that provides for every vote
    counting and every vote being counted

Universal Healthcare and a Living Wage for all

Elected officials with a conscience

And I support most of all

you and the citizens like you all over this city, this
    state, this nation and this world who give a
    damn and make a difference

Memo To James Carville

November 2006

James,

Well, you've gone and done it again. You've made another obvious and rather ineffective attempt at bullying the membership of the Party with your latest rant on who is sitting in the Chair of the Party or whom you think should be. I can only assume that you got your barking orders from Rahm or Chuck or Paul or perhaps it was Bill and Hill? Gosh, maybe you folks at the DLC don't read the papers anymore. Actually most of us don't but we do try to stay informed. I'll tell you what. Here's some news you could use.

Gov. Howard Dean is the Chair of the Party and will remain so, not only as a result of his election by the DNC but by his 50 state plan, which we, the members, applaud and support. The 50 state plan runs counter to the DLC divide & conquer plan, which is eerily reminiscent of the RNC Rovian divide & conquer plan. We agree with Gov. Dean's 50 state plan and take it to the next logical step, let's contest every House & Senate seat. Your cherry picking, arm-twisting, show me the money routine this go round was old school and lame. We Progressives are in this for the whole enchilada, from local school board all the way to the White House.

James, take a memo to your DLC pals; merely raising your voice and demanding that the membership roll over and play dead won't cut it any longer. We've decided that not only is this a big "d" Democratic Party but from now on it's going to be a small "d" democratic party as well.

Lastly, let me say that there is so much more we could talk about, like the definition of a moderate for instance – what is it you are moderately for; civil rights, social justice, poverty, war, peace? – but let's debate instead. Remember, in the information age, ideas are keen and power is horizontal not vertical. So, in the spirit of our new Speaker's tone we should keep this debate civil and inclusive. Instead of expletive laden rants, which we hear that Rahm prefers, let's debate in an open forum and see who represents the people, the membership, and the citizens, the Progressives or the DLC.

So, you get your team together and we'll get ours and let's have a real old-fashioned stem-winding debate. What have you got to lose? You're the big shots; we're just the regular folks, the worker bees, the swarm. Until then, say hello to your good friend, Joe. I hear he was once a Democrat.

Leading "Our" Way
Forward, Together, in the Progressive Movement

By Wayne Williams, Ahjamu Makalani
And Brad Parker

December 2006

Well, here we are Progressive Democrats, sitting on the edge of control, and the responsibility that comes with it. The reigns of power that we have fought so long and hard for, power both within the Party and in Washington is near and brings with it a grave responsibility indeed. Will we use it wisely? Will we advance the "Liberal Ideal"? Will we advance the progressive vision we hold dear in a manner that the American public will not only except, but also embrace?

And what is the progressive vision?

- Out of Iraq now and the end to preemptive war.
- Confront Global Warming with the same passion we sustained to go to the moon in the 1960's.
- Establish a sustainable energy future without extractables (oil, coal, uranium and natural gas).
- Investigate & hold accountable those who committed crimes against our nation and humanity - leading to the impeachment of the President and Vice President if necessary.

- Establish Single Payer Universal Health Care.
- Promote Economic Opportunity and Fairness.
- Eliminate the causes of Poverty and alleviate its effects – begin by establishing a living wage for all.
- Bring back fairness to the regressive tax system.
- Rebuild our infrastructure.
- Reestablish our good name in the world by reestablishing dialogue and global cooperation.
- Keep the Internet open and neutral.
- Remove corruption from the political game by moving towards Public Funding of all elections and making sure those elections are transparent, not corporately owned and controlled - have clear auditable paper trails and access to the ballot box for all citizens.
- Promotion of a wider and more diverse news information infrastructure.
- Institute massive structural Prison and Justice Reform in the American Gulag of jails and prisons – immediately abolish the Death Penalty.

The list goes on and on….

Can we communicate our vision, and conduct our actions in private and in public with the integrity and respect we expected but did not receive from those we have just unseated from power? Or will we act like taciturn, abusive and rambunctious children? Will we rush to judgment without the rest of the nation in agreement with us or will we rationally build consensus by exposing the truth and have the public demand we act in the manner we know is essential? The test is now before us. We will only succeed if we not only speak the truth and expose the injustices but also do it in a manner consistent with "our" ideals and values.

After the election of 2004, we realized it was likely that for the next few years things would get worse and it would become essential that we not panic. We needed to grieve at the theft of our democracy and then act to organize for the future. We needed to be prepared so that when the worst began to happen we could present a bright glowing lighthouse for those who surely would find themselves jumping the sinking ship in the storm coming our way.

Well, we are that lighthouse and all eyes are upon us, the progressives of the Democratic Party who made this victory happen. Make no mistake; our light is now bright and emanating from all 50 states. It was we, the progressives, not the DLC, who won this election - with the aid of a colossal Republican meltdown. We competed everywhere because we were not afraid. We knew in the hearts of America that the people felt as we do, that this nation is not a bully and is capable of great good and decency. Yet, we can extinguish our opportunity for great good easily with divisiveness and actions that reflect our past frustrations. We could easily behave like those we have come to detest. This, we cannot do. This, we must not do. Revenge may feel sweet initially but is a poison that will prove our downfall as it has proven to be to the Republicans. The process we pursue in righting the wrongs of the past dozen years is critical for our long-term well being as a nation.

Let us first say that we know we will succeed in our shared vision. We have no other choice. The nation and our planet can handle nothing less. The question is, will we be respected through the process? Will others learn from our integrity of process and do we have the will to act with respect to others in that process? To facilitate our sense that we can go in such a positive direction we are going to share our thoughts. We hope they will not only touch your minds but also touch your hearts as a guide for action so that our goals may be reached in the most expeditious and legal means possible. After all, we are a nation of laws, are we not?

First, we must expose the fear within us, and all the fear that has driven the success of the Republicans until their glorious defeat of November 7th, 2006. To expose that fear, we must methodically expose the lies and manipulation foisted upon the nation by the President and all of his men. Patience and directness is critical here. No doubt the new Democratic leadership is primed to do this, no matter what they have said publicly in the past. If they are not we are ready to remind them of their duty. Our vigilance is not reserved for one political Party but for all politicians.

When the public sees how they were beguiled and frightened into acting against their own self-interest they will want those responsible held accountable for their deceit. Most Americans have a sense they have been taken for granted and abused but they don't know what we know. So, we must go through the procedure of exposing it through due process. The Radical Right and the Cheney/Bush White House manipulated the public with lies and the public needs to know how and why it happened in order for them to be partners in the repair of the damage done. It is essential we proceed with these steps in an adult process. Acting out of anger and retribution will only build resistance and end in failure.

We must define the code of conduct that will lead us to our common goal of a better world consistent with the understanding, compassion & respect for others we prize so dearly. Don't replicate the actions of those you abhor, as you will surely follow in their footsteps. Remember, you become what you behold. Detach yourself from the hate. Rise above it to your higher awareness. Grow and expand your acceptance of the change that is inevitable. Control is a tool of the past unable to till the vineyards of the future. Facilitation is the new successful paradigm; belligerence is the death of life and the collapse of long-term success in any venture. So let's not fall into the brittle manners of the Republicans. Let's make changes with policy not by maligning any citizen's personality, especially within our own movement. Let us follow the admonition of Dr. Martin Luther King Jr. who told us that: "Darkness cannot drive out darkness; only light can do that. Hate cannot drive out hate; only love can do that."

We must find ways to empower groups and individuals through positive solutions. Feeding on the negative will only galvanize the resentment of others. OK, we know you are sitting there saying, "but we must make them accountable for their actions." We will, have no doubt but the process we move with will decide our long-term success or failure. We like to call it baby steps to positive growth. We build a foundation of support as we go and in the end the walking becomes an organic process empowered not just by our efforts but by the public itself that demands justice. If we have setbacks, we stand again and with our integrity and respect, we move forward again, just like we did after 2000 and 2004.

We must learn to play well the chess game that is politics. Doing so will bring us to our progressive goals of a better more honest world. If we act with respect for not only those with similar dreams - by building strength and respect for others – but by dialogue with those opposed to our propositions, our actions will bring others to us. Then, and only then is anything and everything possible.

We must remain vigilant and respect each other. We are not children in search of parents. We are adults who willingly cooperate with other adults to our mutual benefit. We almost lost our Republic to fascism. Let us not allow, ever again, abusive incompetents, claiming to be all knowing parents, with little awareness of history, to bring our nation and the planet so close to complete destruction. We may still be heading in the wrong direction but we now have our hands on the wheel and we must drive with deliberate care and clarity.

There is so much to be gained by organizing and so much to lose by not organizing and being strident. You will be very surprised how many at the top of the Party are with us. We are growing because our message of enfranchisement, empowerment and veneration for others, regardless of what their station in life may be, has resonated in the collective aspirations of what "Sly and the Family Stone" poignantly called, "everyday people." We are either going to be the Party of inclusion or one that collapses under its self-righteous petulance. No matter how correct we may feel we are, the opinion of others is of equal value. In a democracy all voices must be heard because everyone has something to say that's worth listening to. That's the power of diversity, the strength of consensus.

Being capable of holding those in power accountable comes not by acting like them in their imagined perfection and privilege. It comes by staying true to our ideals, those of the Bill of Rights, the Constitution and due process. If we fail, and demand retribution without first walking the difficult path that investigates and exposes the truth, we will be no different than those we despise and resent.
Let's not become the hypocrites we will soon hold accountable. Let us be proud that we used our power wisely and passed on our respect for this great nation in the process. Let us stand with the

rule of law as we bring to justice those who sought to rend its fabric. Let us stand together, differences and all. E Pluribus Unum.

Wayne Williams is a Board Member of Valley Democrats United and the leader of the media rapid response group Progressive American Citizens / Los Angeles

Ahjamu Makalani is San Bernardino Democratic Party Central Committee First Vice Chair and Vice Chair for California Democratic Party Progressive Caucus

Brad Parker is President of Valley Democrats United, Vice President of Progressive Democrats of Los Angeles and an Officer of the California Democratic Party Progressive Caucus

I Dissent

April 2007

Democrats,

There is a resolution making its way around the state called, "Democrats Working Together to Win in '08." It may be well intentioned but I believe it to be insidious and a feeble but effective attempt at censorship.

Here is my reply to this resolution, which I will oppose at every turn. I am not speaking here on behalf of VDU or its board but for myself. I will deliver these remarks wherever this resolution is introduced.

Unfortunately it was passed at the Los Angeles County Central Committee without discussion or these remarks would have been made there. Here is the resolution, followed by my comments:

> WHEREAS, in our effort to win races at the National, State and local levels inclusive of the 2008 general election and beyond, it is critical that Democrats stay focused, promote unity, and work collaboratively to achieve our goals, and
>
> WHEREAS whether we call ourselves Centrists, Progressives, Liberals, Moderates, or another label, we are all Democrats, and as members of this big-tent-party deserve to be treated with respect and allegiance, whatever our differences, and

WHEREAS rude and intolerant behavior, name-calling and divisive tactics among Democrats do nothing to promote the ideals and success of our Party or to further the cause of small "d" democracy

THEREFORE BE IT RESOLVED that LACDP expects all Democrats to uphold the highest standards of decorum at party meetings, elections, and events, which includes acting respectfully and courteously to each other at all times, and

BE IT FURTHER RESOLVED that LACDP encourages Democratic activists to constructively address intra-party differences through vigorous debate, while staying focused on our mission of electing Democrats and a government of which we can be proud.

Members of the Committee,

I do not owe or swear my allegiance to any political party.

This noble idea, this Republic, was founded on the principle that all citizens are created equal. In order to perfect this union, this social contract, it is the duty of every citizen to give either their informed consent or their fearless dissent.

If any one in this room or this Party or in this nation deems themselves to be worthy of leadership in this Party or in an elected office then they must accept their responsibility to be accountable to the members of this Party and the citizens of the Republic.

Dissent, even rancorous and rude dissent, is our birthright and I will not be intimidated by any member of this Party or any citizen into relinquishing my rights and nor should any of you.

This nation was founded on our unalienable rights to a redress of grievances that culminated in a Revolution.

Never forget that solemn fact.

As a duly elected member of this Party and an officer of several of its bodies, I call upon every member of this body to reject this resolution as a vain attempt to enforce the insidious type of unity rule only found in dictatorships.

I would rather have any person in the Democratic Party be rude to me in a heated debate and even divisive, as so many of us if not all of us are, than to be bound by any allegiance to any person, place or thing other than my own conscience.

This is how the Founders intended it to be and so shall it remain!

Signed

Brad Parker
Valley Democrats United, President
Progressive Democrats of Los Angeles, Vice
President
Progressive Caucus of the CDP, Officer
Delegate to the DSCC, 42nd AD
CDP, Voter Services Committee

Paying the Price

October 2007

Valley Dems,

Thomas Jefferson once remarked that, "the price of freedom is eternal vigilance." Well, nothing has changed except that we have arrived – the Progressive Movement. And in that regard, we must continue to hold every elected official – especially Democrats – accountable for each and every vote and contribution that they take. Fabian Nunez's hubris this past week is ample proof of that. The recalcitrant and catatonic Congress is proof of that. Whomever is the Democratic Party nominee for President in 2008 our job remains the same. Elect a Democrat President and stay on'em 24/7. We must always demand accountability to "We the People." They all – all elected officials and all government bureaucrats – work for us. We must never be afraid to challenge the current leadership of the Democratic Party or the Progressive Movement. In that regard let me begin with myself. Every essay, article or speech I have written or delivered has engendered heated opposition form the current Party leadership or the membership of the Progressives. I always rub somebody the wrong way. Good, I welcome opposition to my propositions. However, don't stop there with me or anyone else who presumes to lead – don't just oppose, make a proposition yourself and let us see where you would lead. That's the beauty of the "swarm" effect in our modern paradigm. The membership is the leadership. We are all leaders! So don't just critique - do something! Write an article. Propose an action. Organize your neighborhood. Energize the body politic with your passion. Remember – there is no easy walk to freedom. Keep the free speech, the positive action and the heated debate flowing. Together – "We" might just make this American Experiment work after all....

Stand Up, Show Up, Speak Up, Act Now, Vote!!!!

further...

Brad Parker
President, Valley Democrats United

Bad Mojo Rising

July 2008

A malevolent cloud is sweeping across America tonight. It has permeated the air with betrayal and cowardice. Around the District of Columbia, our putative leaders are breathing in the foul stench of capitulation and finding it to not be as nauseating as they imagined it would be. Our fearsome and feckless Democratic Senate is poised on the precipice of utter degradation. Tomorrow, July 10, 2008, a majority of Democrats in the Senate will march in robotic step with a majority of Democrats in the House and drag our Party, the Constitution and our Republic into the gutter of craven careerism with gusto and enthusiasm. They will vote for the abridged FISA act and gut the Constitution.

Our venerable "Fourth Amendment" - *The right of the people to be secure in their persons, houses, papers, and effects, against unreasonable searches and seizures, shall not be violated, and no Warrants shall issue, but upon probable cause, supported by Oath or affirmation, and particularly describing the place to be searched, and the persons or things to be seized* - will be immolated on the floor of the Senate in the name of "National Security", which of course will then be impossible to preserve because our "freedom" is our "security". The stench of this massacre of reason and truth will not be cleansed from our Party for decades to come, let alone from the carpet on the Senate floor.

Oh yes, we know the exhausted elucidations of pragmatic exigency that will be paraded before us - spewing from every mass media outlet - by earnest apologists for the prevaricating "centrist" Democrats. We can see their bloviating bobble heads rising in the mojo mist of dawn even now as we drift off to dream of terrors yet to come. They'll smugly chortle, "It was the best compromise we could get" or, "Politics is the art of the possible" or perhaps, "There are Islamic Jihadists in our midst!" It will all be lies, disingenuous lies, and damnable disingenuous lies. They will all do it to save their phony baloney jobs. They don't fear any "terrorists." These recreant cardboard politicians are afraid they will lose their job and all of the bloated perks that come with it - healthcare, pensions, per diem, staff, travel, dinners, country clubs etc. - all of the perks we pay for and they deny us. Therein, dear friends, lies the problem.

One last act before the curtain: will our presumptive Presidential nominee stand for us or lie prostrate before the heel of the tyrants Cheney and Bush? Which Democratic patriots, among the cowering 100, will rail against this pulverizing of the, "flag for which it stands for" into nanodust suitable for sweeping under the rug or mounting on a lapel pin? Mark their names fellow Americans; those few who brave the siren call of the incumbency circus. For these are the last representatives left in D.C., from the proud liberal ideal, the New Deal, the Great Society and the Democratic Party. In the dark years to come they will need our help.

So Democrats, if you have ever questioned the need for a Progressive Movement, there will be no better demonstration of its undeniable necessity in our lifetimes than this promenade of submission. Our ancestors are rising from their graves to demand of us the strength to deny this groveling cabal their complete usurpation of our inherent rights and independence. Heed the call. Never capitulate to the clamor for silence and complicity. King George Bush has committed high crimes against America and humanity and the Democratic Congress is aiding and abetting him in this latest illegal act. Will he ever be brought to justice? Will no Democratic leader stop him?

Do not accept the specious narration being offered by Democratic Party leaders, electeds or consultants that the dying light of our Republic and our Party is actually a bright new flame of change. Resist the woeful songs of the gradualists and incrementalists, who claim they are on our side but we will have to wait. Remember July 10, 2008. There's a bad mojo rising. It not only comes from the Republican Anarchy Collective but from the heart of the Democratic Party. And that is the reason for the Progressive Swarm to renew its commitment to our cause - a Progressive Democratic Party and majority in America. Stand up for your rights. Show up and demand change in the Democratic Party. Speak up whenever and wherever possible and never let anyone shut you up!

Spread the Word.

Stand Up!

PART IV

Progressive Voice

Liberally Speaking
(Or Gag me with a Wiretap)

March 2006

Three hundred years ago an American patriot was born who wrote, "They that can give up essential liberty to obtain a little temporary safety deserve neither liberty nor safety." I'm sure that Benjamin Franklin wouldn't have been surprised by how many times in American history there would be attempts to do just that.

First came the "Alien & Sedition Acts" of 1798 then the "Suspension of Habeas Corpus" in 1861. There was the "House Committee on Un-American Activities" from 1945 to 1975 and the infamous "COINTELPRO" from 1956 to 1971. All of these actions were designed to deny "Freedom of Speech" and "Assembly" guaranteed in the Constitution and Bill of Rights. All were eventually discredited.

It's no surprise to us that King George, our current tyrant occupying both the White House and Iraq has made the vain attempt to do it once again. Ever the clever lad, "W" has decided to wiretap, surveil and detain any American citizen whom he chooses for no reason at all, without a warrant or court or legal preceding. Along with his so-called "strict-constructionist" cabal of sooth-sayers, he has divined words in the Constitution heretofore unseen. To protect us from evildoers at home and spread democracy abroad he has declared that the Constitution gives him "Inherent Rights" that supercede our "Unalienable Rights." We can assume that his Crown is under construction at Tiffany's and being readied for the declaration of Marshall Law.

Confronted by a swarm of citizens, even some members of the press, he told us that well if isn't in the Constitution then it's in the "2001 Authorization of Military Force." No, replied a browbeaten Congress, it's not in there.

So, with that clueless dry-drunk grin, Shrub finally said, "You'll just have to trust me." Well George, we don't. No more than the folks you flew over in New Orleans. More importantly, we aren't afraid of you either. You and the Corporate misanthropes who have the Establishment Democrats and Republicans so enthralled in DC are finished but you don't know it. Like the Music business discovered, the genie is out of the bottle. It's called the "Internet," and with it we are organizing from the grassroots up. We are the future. You vertical power players are yesterday. It's a new beautiful, horizontal, citizens-first, bottom-up world of politics powered by the seamless person-to-person connection of the World Wide Web.

Hey, you members of the DLC "hackocracy," don't you get it? We'll send you an email. You can go back to sleep now. And remember… don't Breakdown… Breakthrough

The Evolution will be Realized…

Despair, Hope and the Digital Democracy
(Editorial on Lila Garret's "Connect the Dots"
On KPFK)

May 2006

Hello, I'm Brad Parker...

Out of the shock of September 11, 2001 the Bush administration hyped the climate of fear to promote a long-standing goal of the radical right; imperialize the world. Like so many tyrants before him, Bush declared that he would bring peace and freedom to the world by waging unending war, beginning in Iraq. Cheney, Rumsfeld, Rove and the Republican masters of the Black Arts of Deceit manipulated 9/11 to justify their goal of an unchecked executive branch. For far too many Americans, paralyzed by the steady drumbeat of terror and fear, despair has set in. But hope has arrived. Let me tell you about it.

Across the Nation, the Internet has given us the greatest toolbox for change we have ever known. In the 60's we organized in the street. Today we organize on the World Wide Web. In the 60's the most effective tool for organizing was the print medium. Today? Its' cell phones and PDA's, email and instant messaging, web sites and blogs and podcasts and in a word its' "digital." The pyramid of power and leadership has been turned upside down.

Those of us at the bottom, you know, the citizens, can now speak directly to each other. Then we all meet up, go out and effect change. Finally, no more middle man from the macro-media or party leadership filtering our information. Micro-media has made, as Thomas Friedman said, the world flat with a very broad horizon. The informed consent of the citizenry hailed by Jefferson is on the rise. To all of you vertical power players, adios.

And so I say to you: If you are mired in despair or outrage dare to nourish your hope. Take the office of citizenship seriously. Join your local Democratic Club. Join your local chapter of a National Organization dedicated to Liberal and Progressive values. Become a delegate to your State

Democratic Party. Be a participant in democracy not just an observer or critic.

The Despair of War is a result of the failure of narrow self-interest. The Hope of Peace will be the result, as Lincoln said, of the better angels of our nature and even though much more difficult to achieve, it is our destiny. Using this powerful "digital" technology we will drive the inertia of despair from our democracy with the actions of hope.

So, Act. Act Now. Act for Peace. Act for Justice. Act for all.

Thanks for listening and remember…
Don't Breakdown… Breakthrough

Why are we here?

May 2006

We ask ourselves today... **why are we here?**
What is the purpose of "our" Progressive Caucus
in the CDP
We are here because we find ourselves like the
citizens of NO
    In the Superdome and
    In the Convention Center
"On Our Own"
No one is coming to save us
Leaders from the past are either rich
    Or worse; consumed by indifference
They are not coming to save us
They no longer believe that the Democratic Party
is viable
The Democratic Party has been abandoned by the
people
The Democratic Party is held in disdain by the
vast Liberal majority
They have voted by staying away from the polls in
droves
And so here we are
We few who still believe

Corporations have sucked the blood out of the
Republican Party
Its' corpse is beginning to rot
Under corporate direction it is now the
    Republican Anarchy Collective
Busy dismantling every level of government
Creating a world run by self-interested fanatics
replacing

Science with **Superstition**
Environmental Protection with **Pollution**
Business regulation with **robber barons**
Public Education with **Private Segregation**
War without End
Anarchy, chaos and poverty for the overwhelming majority
Gated, guarded, gaudy lifestyles for the very few

Corporate Crony Capitalism has now turned its' sights on Elected Democrats…
Beginning in the 1990's a concerted campaign has been waged to convert the DNC into the other wing of the
National Corporate Party
Led by the **DLC** they have found our weakness…
money
Money that can buy re-election
Money that can lift a middle class activist with good intentions
Out of the neighborhood and into the world of privilege

Too many times at every level of government we have found Democrats doing the bidding of **Corporate Lobbyists** under the banner of **Jobs**…
They tell us we have to sacrifice our principles or we won't have any **jobs**… so they sacrifice in our name and all we get is **fewer and fewer lousy jobs**…

We are here to bring a **conscience** to the Democratic Party
We know that California is the ultimate prize in the political future
As goes California, so goes the nation, the world

We are here to **transform the CDP** and then the **DNC** will follow

We are here to support all of our elected officials who are doing the right thing and elect more like them

We are here to give those who are not… the opportunity to see the error of their ways and regain their moral compass

We are here to inspire those who have abandoned the political process to join us because every challenge before us in America today is being decided in the political arena and we cannot leave the process to only the corrupt corporate influences and to the weak politicians who succumb to them

We are the foundry of ideas. Our focus should be policy not personality. Our action should be keen. Our by-word should be inclusion. You are the leadership of the Progressive Caucus. Make sure you elect an Executive Board who understands that!

I ask for your support

(Speech given at the 2006 CDP Progressive Caucus elections)

 Internet Integrity

Preserve the Integrity of the Internet
as an open, fair and accessible
forum for ideas, speech and business.

The Internet is public property
benefiting the public good much like the
Interstate Highway System.

Don't allow the Internet to be privatized
and turned into a toll road
where the few dictate to the many,
what they can see, hear and buy.

Tell your representatives
at every level of government to
**vote for permanent
Net Neutrality**

*(Written in support of the CDP Net Neutrality
Resolution – August 2007)*

Show Up!

PART V

America Redux

Holier Than Thou
(Theocracy vs. Democracy)

April 2003

In every corner of the globe there are movements to unseat or retain control of governments by the "Holier Than Thou" brigades of the theocrats. Some of these movements are opposed to tyrants some are the tyrants. Rather than offering freedom, they are trying to impose just another lame autocratic shell game and rob the citizens of their unalienable rights. Theocracy is in a grudge match with democracy. Thanks to some "deists" in the eighteenth century British colonies of North America though, the die is cast, the outcome is already clear. Even so, religion will not give up easily to logic and reason. Fundamentalism, in all of its religious forms, is the last staunch bastion of patriarchy. Theocracy is the last stand of the political patriarchy. Old ways will continue to grasp to power. However, only the secular state can lead the way to democracy.

Maybe what appeals to so many about the secular state is the new playing field. When the man, and it always seems to be a man, at the front of the room has a direct connection to God - he runs the show. In a democracy, each citizen is enfranchised by his or her creator - whomever that creator may be. When God becomes directly connected to everyone in the room, it becomes more difficult to arbitrarily tell people what to do, what to think. In a state run by a man with a secret link to the truth, who can tell what the truth really is? In a state run by women and men all searching for the common truth it may never be known but they will do immeasurably more good in the meantime. "E Pluribus Unum" was more to the point as a motto for this nation than "In God We Trust." It is harder to control but infinitely more productive. Not to say, that a secular democracy can't cause harm, it can, but in a secular democracy there is at least a chance of reform and a reversal of onerous policy. The Vietnam War and the Civil Rights struggles of 20th century America are good examples of this.

Only the secular state can guarantee the freedom to practice any and all religions by not preferring or establishing any one in particular. Power in the secular state comes from the bottom up not the top down as in a theocracy. When the base of power is solid, then the people at the top will have a better view of what is and what should be. Theocracy cannot even guarantee the unfettered practice of the state religion. Apostates will always abound. Our Founders understood that by separating church and state both are strengthened. They also understood that the state must not then become the master of the citizens. Even in a secular democracy centralized power at the top will undermine citizen's rights. The consent of the governed is the essential operating principle for any government from this point forward.

Communism failed because it replaced theocracy with autocracy not democracy. Democracy was never possible in that arrangement because the new was merely the old with a different name and face. Old religion was replaced by new. The state became the new religion. A tyrant at the top was the new man at the front of the room. Cult of personality replaced cult of icons. As with any dictatorship, once again the top down theory of power was unstable and doomed. Without consent and consensus, communism was unsustainable. Communism also quashed the freedom to create wealth and hold private property, as does a theocracy. Without the freedom to aspire and attain in the marketplace, human beings are a miserable lot. Only a secular democracy can guarantee that freedom.

Many have tried to corrupt or distort our Founders vision for humanity since 1776. All have failed. Why? Because this vision, this experiment, is an idea whose time has come. Perhaps the end of states controlled by religion, anywhere on the globe, will breed a new spirituality. Perhaps a deeper more profound faith will arise from the true core of all the world's religious practices raised in the fertile soil of secular democracy. Maybe in this new faith, there will be an understanding of each other - a trust. When the many do become one, then maybe, just maybe, "God Will Trust Us".

I'll Take That
(Or how I learned to stop occupying other countries and love the Internet)

May 2003

As the MWD dust settles over Baghdad, the neo-cons will be wondering where to go next in their empire building. Much to their dismay they will be too late to go anywhere. The colonial era of world politics, which stretches back to our very origins, is on the wane. Information is the enemy of the neo-cons; the anarchists and all would be Big Brothers. Bits and bytes of information are breaking down all social orders that preceded them. Instead of enslaving people, as George Orwell predicted, the emerging technological environment is becoming an instrument of liberation. It is in fact, becoming the new world order.

Colonialism, the domination and exploitation of one nation or group by another, has run its course. Nationalism, like the organizational paradigms before it, will become less stifling as each corner of the globe becomes a partner and participant with every other corner. Digital information carried silently worldwide over the Internet is blurring all national boundaries. A "Global Village" will be less tolerant of oppression no matter where it is occurring. Every countries issues will become all countries issues. How long can it be before it blurs all corporate boundaries? All cultural boundaries? Is this a good thing? I think it is.

The music industry is the first corporate world to collapse, a little over a decade after the fall of the Soviet Empire. The Soviet Union was undermined by information carried on VCR tapes past the government and directly into the homes of the citizens. The world on tape beat the lies on the TV and in the press. Just as that information did, the World Wide Web has finished off an aging, bloated and lazy music industry. While ripping off the artists and consumers with a stranglehold on the availability of recordings, (i.e. colonial domination), a new technology broke through the old boys network of record and publishing companies. The industry was undermined by consumer sharing of existing music (one step ahead of new regulations) and by a flood of new musical ideas from around the world, shared on the Internet. Greed and a lack of foresight on the part of many music business executives sped on the demise. A new music "business" has arisen (i.e. legal downloads via the Internet ala Apple's iTunes) and the old one is dead or dying. Digital information did it in. All nations, all industries are being reformed by information. Any attempt by the major players in geopolitics to maintain or regain control will be futile. Any attempt by anarchists to destroy or distort relationships will be treated as a disease and quickly attacked by the white blood cells of information and mutual interests. America, the current dominant power economically, militarily and culturally, cannot achieve or sustain hegemony over the globe. Other nations are in less of a position to do so. Terrorists are even further out of the loop. Information is becoming our friend.

Marshall McLuhan's global village will be in fact,

a quilt of many decentralized villages that are all intertwined by the World Wide Web. All forms of information and communication will synergize into one large multilingual library available through ever increasing multiple electronic devices, on demand worldwide. Instead of forming one indistinct humanity, it will celebrate all of the myriad diversities and marvelous differences globally. The ubiquitous interconnection will create the reverse of Big Brother. People will be watching who is watching them. This will make it more and more difficult for the powers that be to get away with murder or theft, whether on a local, regional or global scale. Of course, owing to human weakness there will still be enough slackers, hackers and attackers to keep us all vigilant. That won't change. However, colonization and domination of one group by another will be increasingly more difficult to operate. The rule of peoples by class, religion, gender or ideology will become more suspect as the media explores the story and shines the light on previously hidden practices. Even though hierarchies will still exist as in the past, as well as the impulse for anarchy among the disillusioned, the poor and the opportunists, slowly the bits and bytes of information, like flies at the waste dump, will break it all down, composting it, allowing something new and unexpected to appear. Something wonderful is at work.

The War On drUgS
(Culture War I)

October 2004

Across the globe tonight our enemy is plotting our demise. With every victory in our effort, their hardcore remnants become more determined. We have mobilized our Armed Forces, our Police, our CIA, our FBI, our INS and our Homeland Security against this real and present danger. Or have we? Every resource we posses may be necessary in this global conflict. So, what are we doing fighting an un-winnable, ill-advised and pointless "War On Drugs," when the very real enemy is amongst and against us? Let's examine this dilemma from two points of view. One - what is the "War On Drugs"? Two - can we afford it while we are at war with our very real and tangible enemies, i.e. Radical Islamists and White Supremacists (remember Oklahoma City?) as well religious, political and economic extremists around the globe?

The inaccurately named "War On Drugs" is a recent phenomenon. It should correctly be called the "War On Us." We can find no reference to it in any of the documents, which founded our Republic. For the century following the birth of the nation, we find no legal precedents identifying and making drugs illegal. Somewhere in the late 19th and early 20th century religious fundamentalists, in this case "Christian," got up in arms about perceived moral decay. Over the following decades, more and more behavior was deemed "bad" by these moral police. Alcohol, prostitution, drugs and gambling were systematically outlawed in most of the country. No one can deny the dangers in these behaviors; why then did not the founders banish them at the conception of the nation? They all certainly existed at the time. The answer is "FREEDOM." These matters are among the powers reserved for the people in Amendment Ten of the Constitution. Every one of these activities is a question of personal behavior, not a legal or criminal matter. These adult activities were certainly around at the time but were thought of as moral not criminal decisions. Our forbearers left the decision on these matters up to the individual not the government.

The watershed era for "moral" legislation on drugs was the 1950s, 60s and early 70s. A country divided fought with itself on the great issues of war and peace, race and justice, gender and equality. Perhaps feeling humiliated by the social victories of the left on Civil Rights, against the War in Vietnam and for a woman's right to choose, the fundamentalist right pushed the "War On Drugs." The "Culture War," as Justice Scalia so aptly referred to it, was on. Over thirty misguided years of misery, injustice, massive corruption and financial waste have followed.

In every home, on TV and radio, in magazines and newspapers and on the Internet, more and more drugs and cure-alls are pushed, hawked and pitched to the American public every day. Drug companies make billions on these nostrums, said to bring instant relief from every known malady common to humans. Listen to any right-wing radio talk show or so-called "liberal biased" evening network newscast if you want to hear and see how many drugs we are being sold every minute of every day. Now, even mental or emotional anguish can be subsumed by a clever little pill or "medicine," as the people who sell it prefer that you call it.

It is inconceivable that a nation force-fed drugs as the answer to every problem of the day would be able to differentiate among "bad" and "good" drugs. There are more dangerous drugs sold over the counter than on the black market, just ask Rush Limbaugh. If prohibition of alcohol couldn't work why would prohibition of "certain" drugs? It's time to give up the charade. We can't afford this war. We can't win it. "We" are the enemy in this war. A true enemy is laughing while we fight this war and not them. It's time to wake up.

Much to the credit of several Republican leaders – George Schultz, Gov. Gary Johnson, Milton Freidman and William F. Buckley Jr. among them – the devastating economic costs have been brought to light. Illegal substances have corrupted and undermined countries around the world as well as too many American police departments and all of the government agencies designed to stop them. Just like Prohibition, they have not stopped any behaviors; they have only created cartels of gangsters and fed money to terrorists. Yes, one of the major sources of money to all terrorists groups is the money from the production and sale of "illegal" drugs. These illegal markets have undermined nations - i.e. Afghanistan, Morocco, Pakistan, Columbia, Bolivia, Mexico, and Myanmar etc. - leading to military dictatorships, general chaos and corruption. In America, police, courts and civic institutions have been drowned in a quagmire of corruption and lost revenue for pointless enforcement of these bogus laws. It costs $30,000 a year on average to incarcerate a youth or send them to college. Which one do you prefer? It's time to decriminalize, legalize, educate, regulate and rehabilitate. Drugs are a health problem not a criminal problem.

The only way to stop the destruction is to end the war. When will Democratic leaders get over their lack of courage and tell the truth about this useless "War On Us"? Are they afraid of being tainted, tarred and feathered by the people on the other side of the Culture War? Get over it. Stand up for who you were and who you are. The freedom to choose your behavior is not a tacit endorsement of any behavior. It's a call to responsibility for your own person, the original private property. Pursuing the un-winnable "War On Us" will lead to losing the war against radical fundamentalist terror. We can't afford both.

It's time to grow up, give personal responsibility back to the individual and get about solving the real problems in the world. Democrats should be leading this struggle not cowering in the shadows.

When the so-called illegal drugs are put back into the same category as the prescription and over-the-counter drugs, then we can tax, regulate and deflate the money in the market for all drugs. We can stabilize the nation's police departments and other government agencies involved in drug prosecution by taking the money out of the equation. We can put the resources of the DEA et al to work on Homeland Security, not the citizenry. We can empty at least half of the prisons. We must rehabilitate the addicts who can be reached and take the users and abusers out of prison and put them in clinics. An end to the over-inflated black market will bring normalcy. At the same time, we must educate all citizens about the powerful dangers of <u>all</u> drugs.

If we can live with the dangers of guns and cars and alcohol then the dangers of drugs can be handled as well.

The government is not the proper place to correct or direct moral behavior. If your family, faith or community cannot positively influence your behavior, no law will be effective in the attempt to do so. Some people will always fall down. If they can be put back together, then we should. If they can't, then as a last resort separate them from the public in a "hospital" not a prison. The government would serve us all better by concentrating on the behavior of the "boardroom" not the "bedroom."

What would the result of freeing up all of these precious resources be? They could be put to use rebuilding our fractured communities and fighting our current and real enemies including Radical Islamists and White Supremacists as well religious, political and economic extremists around the globe. Wake up Democrats! It's time to tell the truth and change the nation and the world for the betterment of all of us. It's time for a Democratic leader to emerge, who has the guts to lead - not make excuses.

LIBERATING THE LIBERALS
(How not to be Conned, Cowered or Co-opted)

January 2005

Amid the hand wringing of the Democrats, wandering in the wilderness of monumental defeat, crying "We were robbed", "We must embrace Moral Values", "Capitulate to the Right" and "Everybody into the Middle of the Road", we should take the time to pause and reflect on how we got to this place and just who we really are - Liberals.

According to the Encarta World English Dictionary "liberal" is defined as:

lib·er·al, adjective
- *tolerant of different views and standards of behavior in others*
- *favoring gradual reform, especially political reforms that extend democracy, distribute wealth more evenly, and protect the personal freedom of the individual*
- *relating to a political ideology of liberalism*
lib·er·al, noun
somebody who favors tolerance or reform

Now I ask you, where is the problem with that? Of course, there is none. However, for the last three decades both it's adherents and detractors have done all they can to redefine or eventually obliterate the term "Liberal" from our political lexicon and the Democratic Party. Their reasoning has followed three main premises:

1. The **CON**: European American Males (White Men) and their interests should form the main platform of the Democratic Party and these same men should fill the primary positions of the Party hierarchy because the largest voting block in America is "White Men" and they have the highest voter turnout, especially in the South.

2. The **COWER**: Everyone knows that LIBERAL = SOCIALIST = COMMUNIST = SATAN. (This old canard was made coin of the realm by 30 years of Republican disinformation and the FOX news network)

3. The **CO-OPT**: Now that you've made a lot of money, your interests lay with the ownership class not the working class.

Let's examine these schools of thought and reveal the hollow shell behind their glitzy façade.

The "CON" gained purchase within the ranks of our party with the advent of the Democratic Leadership Council. The DLC premise is; only "White Men" vote so let's drop everything and just go after their votes. They arrived at their premise after the flight of the Dixiecrats to the Republican ranks and the loss of traction with "White Male" voters in general. On the face of it, it seemed plausible but the plan failed miserably (an outcome which some of us at the time accurately predicted). Why would "White Men" vote Democrat when all of their fears and prejudices (not to mention their greed) were being catered to by the Republicans who are mostly "White Men" like them? Obviously, they wouldn't and they didn't, in droves. All the "White Men" have already decided where they stand and for most it's with the Republicans. Hence, no White house, no Congress, few State Houses etc. etc. etc. And to add insult to injury, while the DLC chased the "White Guys" the Democrats lost votes with women, minorities, young voters and even unions, all, our natural and historic constituencies. Karl Rove knew we were running away from our base and he successfully went after it. After 12 years of losses in election cycles (other than Bill Clinton) they should replace the word "leadership" with "loser." The DLC changed nothing, lost much and yet remains in control of our party. The emperor has no clothes. It's time for the DLC to go.

The "COWER" is based on a formula that is equally false no matter which way you work it. LIBERAL = SOCIALIST = COMMUNIST = SATAN is no more true than CONSERVATIVE = CAPITALIST = FASCIST = SATAN. These "Big Lies" were devised to dehumanize political opponents. Non-humans can be dealt with ruthlessly. These lies are expedient for pols with an axe to grind and no patience for reason or compromise. What happened to the concepts of civil discourse and the loyal opposition? Many liberals say, "They trash us so let's trash them." That's not very productive. We need to be true to our principles, which include tolerance and understanding, no matter what tactics they take. You can't get lower than the Swifties even when you try. Some liberals say, "Let's be Progressives." A rose by any other name is still a rose. Why should we run away from our traditions and accomplishments? Let's turn around and make a stand. If Ronald Reagan can rehabilitate the term "Conservative" what's wrong with our leadership? The term "Liberal," as the definition shows, is worth fighting for.

The "CO-OPT" is the most insidious chain being drug around by liberals. "Limousine Liberal" is an apt term to describe this crowd. You know who they are. They trumpet their Democratic values but in the workplace and in their private lives they act as Republicans. They are... you and I. We struggled to make it to the top of our profession or we inherited our fortune and sense of noblese oblige. We have our homes in the toney neighborhoods. We have our children in the best schools. We have our private beach property. We attend the best charity events. We make socially aware products. We changed the world. Or did we? We also have our illegal alien nannies and housekeepers and gardeners and cooks. We own or invest in businesses that hire other illegal aliens at sub-human wages. We support Prop. 13 to keep the tax rate low for our business interests in the guise of keeping old folks in their little homes. We are PRO business just like Gov. Schwarzenegger, at a great cost to those who have little or nothing. We are against foreign wars but invest in the industries that profit from them. We turn a blind eye to the disgrace of doing business with China, the largest slave labor camp on the planet. We talk like Democrats but walk like Republicans. We are a sham, just a bunch of middle class folks crawling over each other to get to the country club.

It's time to stop hiding from the truth. The Sixties were not the destruction of American values they were the fulfillment. It was liberals and their true conservative allies who stopped the travesty of the Vietnam War. It was liberals and their true conservative allies who championed and won Civil Rights for all Americans. It was liberals and their true conservative allies who brought about a new consciousness of the planet we all inhabit and how to care for it. It was liberals and their true conservative allies who promoted the idea of our inalienable right to personal freedom, especially women's reproductive rights. It was liberals and their true conservative allies who blazed the path out of poverty for millions of Americans. And, it was liberals and their true conservative allies who redefined spiritual belief in a manner that encompasses all faiths with tolerance and compassion for all sentient beings. We are those liberals.

We must liberate ourselves from illusions, delusions and collusions. We must get a grip, get a backbone, walk tall and define ourselves, not leave it to others. We know that environmental protection and enhancement is not only good for business, it is the best and only sustainable business model. Let's put the green in the greenbacks. We know that women, minorities and youth are the future if not current majority, our majority. Let's stop chasing our tails and go after the future not the past. We know that our accomplishments are interdependent upon the most needy and least among us. We know that we are no better than how we care for them. We know that the treatment of women is the barometer of a free society. After the Taliban, can we deny this? Let us not be the generation that hands over the gains of a liberal society, who so many have struggled and died for, to virulent superstitions from the past. Let's accept that even if we didn't want him to run, Ralph was right; corporations are not more important than citizens. We must rediscover ourselves, our truth. We stand for life, "liberty" and the pursuit of happiness, liberal society, liberal democracy and the Liberal Ideal. Remember? We must all join together and resurrect our cause under the banner "Liberal" and re-take our Party. If this cannot happen in America, how can it happen anywhere in the world? We have work to do.

So, the next time you're driving to your vacation home in your gas guzzling SUV, remember; you can run but you can't hide. Come home. Come back to your roots. Say it loud – I'M LIBERAL AND I'M PROUD!!!

TOP BANANA
(Democracy, Tyranny and the Vote)

March 2005

After a tense campaign, the results are finally in: the winner lost the popular vote but will be installed forthwith as our new leader. It has been a triumph for liberty, freedom and democracy. Of whom do we speak? Palestine? Afghanistan? Ukraine? Iraq? Lebanon? NO - Welcome to the Banana Republic of the United States of America. Perhaps that statement is an exaggeration but only if you are a citizen of this country whose feelings are hurt by the facts. From the outside, we appear to be just that to most of our fellow world citizens - a colossal and oppressive hypocrisy. To them, we preach but we don't practice. If you have an objection to this statement, consider this: Banana Republic is a term most often used to describe a corrupt nation, controlled by outside business interests who pay for the installation and maintenance of a sham government. These governments hold regular elections, which are rigged to uphold the regime, stifle dissent and give the appearance of democracy. These governments deny their citizens the right to a duly elected government based on a one-person-one-vote system. The main function of the government is to provide cheap labor, low costs of doing business and a laissez faire environment for the rich getting richer. Sound familiar? China may be the prime example of this but American voting procedures have much in common with Banana Republics and produce many of the same results.

President Bush has proclaimed a bold new initiative to bring "Freedom, Liberty and Democracy" to the entire world. If he has read the Bible lately, he might remember that passage about removing the beam from your own eye before you remove the speck from another's eye. We may have, to paraphrase Winston Churchill, a flawed system but better than all the rest. However, there's no need to rest on our laurels. We are a long way from every vote counting and every vote counted. You might say we are the "Top Banana."

Most obviously flawed is the procedure for electing the President. Unlike many of the other 118 democracies in the world, we do not have direct election of the highest office in the land. Instead, we have the infamous Electoral College. Our founders got many things right in the Constitution and some very important things wrong. George W. Bush did not win a plurality of the votes cast in 2000. If 120,000 more people had voted for John F. Kerry in 2004 - then he, like Bush, would have won the Electoral College and become President while losing the popular vote. Would Democrats have gloated? Would turn-a-bout have been fair play? If your answer is yes, then you are a knave, who only seeks personal gain to the detriment of all generations of Americans to come. Who can honestly say that they are in favor of a system that rewards the loser? Should the same principle hold true on a State or County or City level then? Why not? If the principle is sound, then why isn't it the law at every level? The further you pursue this misbegotten law the more it stands democracy on its head. The usual defense of the Electoral College is that the small states would have no power in Washington D.C., if there were a direct vote. In fact, without the Electoral College the small states would get more attention. With elections at the national level increasingly split down the middle, the pols would have to go rural to get every last vote and every vote would at last count. It is also alleged that open direct elections would allow splinter parties to force runoffs and things would become very messy. How much bigger of a mess than what we have in D.C. now? Welcome to "democracy." The Electoral College is ludicrous and an embarrassment to all of us. Why hasn't anyone challenged the constitutionality of the Electoral College? Is this a one-person-one-vote electoral system or not? If you reply that, well, you see it's in the original document, so was legal slavery. As Jefferson, the slaveholder said, the Constitution is a living document and should be challenged by every generation for relevancy. Most of its articles will hold up, the Electors provision of Section 1, Article II and Amendment XII, will not. It is time for direct elections of all offices at all levels. Or, are we merely a Banana Republic after all?

Another blight on our voting system is voter suppression. Voter suppression is as old as voter registration and usually begins right there by making registration as difficult as possible. That's as old as Jim Crow at least. However, there are so many other clever ways to go about it. In the last two election cycles, we've had fake voter registration drives in Nevada, disqualified provisional ballots in Ohio, voter intimidation and challenges at the poles in Florida, hanging chads, electronic voting machines with no paper trail, too few voting machines, too few polling stations and the list goes on and on. Who benefits from these felonious tactics? Common wisdom says the Republicans. Maybe that's true but there is a far more insidious tactic for voter suppression that's as old as the Republic - "Get Out The Vote" campaigns - and it benefits both parties. Most citizens participate in "GOTV" campaigns in earnest but the higher up the party ladder you go, the less enthusiasm you find. In real politic, both parties only want the people who will keep them in office to show up. As anyone knows who has worked in them, neither party wants to "GOTV" because if everyone did show up, then they would throw the bums out. Think about it. Women, minorities and young people had to struggle mightily to win the right to vote but that has not translated into much encouragement from either party to show up and vote. All we get is lip service and lame public announcements.

In the final analysis, making it difficult to vote helps maintain the status quo for both parties. Oh yes, and if we are honest with ourselves we have to admit that the greatest of all voter suppression techniques is, "voter apathy." That's where we, the voters, do our part to keep the same old thing going. Maybe this type of voter suppression works best for both parties. It certainly does in a Banana Republic.

Most curious among voting irregularities is voter fraud. Democrat's hands are not clean on this account; remember Chicago in 1960? Did Kennedy really win? And, what of the current variations of fraud? Who was it that registered so many cartoon characters, dead people and other imaginary voters in so many states this time around? No matter, it was fraud in any case. Delusional operatives, believing they are helping their cause by tainting the entire process, are a detriment to us all. Now, that is a Banana Republic at its very best.

Finally, there is, as Jesse Unruh once said, the mother's milk of politics, "money." A cloud of money from the well-heeled and all-powerful business interests, obscuring reasoned thought and civil discourse, sweeps across the land. Our current California Governor, Arnold Schwarzenegger, would have you believe that the true special interests corrupting the system are nurses and teachers and lawyers and unions. President Bush is promoting this idea as well and with the cleverness of Karl Rove, they are both having their day with the media. We are told to cut off the welfare mothers, public education, lawsuits and the elderly's medical coverage and then privatize everything. We are provoked and mobilized to destroy the government because it is our enemy! Then, the market will take care of us all. Let's return to the glory days of the robber barons they say, when government was run like a business. Orwell would have been proud of these boys, wrapping "Tyranny" in the flag of "Democracy." However, Republicans and the Democrats who talk and act like them would be well advised to remember that America is not a corporation. Coolidge was wrong, the business of America is not business. And if it were a business the current management would have to be fired. America is an ideal; *"We the People of the United*

States, in Order to form a more perfect Union, establish Justice, insure domestic Tranquility, provide for the common defence, promote the general Welfare, and secure the Blessings of Liberty to ourselves and our Posterity, do ordain and establish this Constitution for the United States of America", not a slick ad campaign for the preeminence of corporate capitalism. An atmosphere of intense money in political ads gives wealthy people and corporations (the real special interests) many more de facto votes than ordinary citizens. Only "Clean Money Campaign Financing" can stop this brutal dismantling of the true democratic progress, achieved over the last two centuries, in this nation. Or, if you would prefer, we can continue to allow the Banana Republic to flourish at our expense.

So, what then must we do? First, we should stop slapping ourselves on the back for being the most free, most democratic and most advanced democracy on the planet. OK, so we don't have a king and the church doesn't make laws (not that they wouldn't like to!) but we have a long way to go to fulfill the democratic vision cherished by free thinkers ever since Athens was founded. Every time you go to an ATM anywhere in the nation, it knows who you are, it gives you a paper receipt and it connects you to the national mainframe in seconds. Why hasn't this been done for elections? The incidence of fraud in ATMs is well below that of the Presidential elections with many more transactions on any given day. The Constitution says that the Presidential Election is to be on the first Tuesday of November every four years. Why isn't that a national holiday so that voters have all day to cast their vote? There are so many ways to improve our system that you must ask yourself why they haven't been done. The answer is obvious: why would the foxes protect the chicken coop, when they have a 95% incumbency re-election rate and are free to raid the chicken coop at will? Why indeed.

We are drowning in an antiquated and deeply flawed voting system that does not work. We, the voters, are lazy and indifferent and that's exactly what both parties want. Most elected officials are only concerned with keeping their current position or eyeing the next one that they aspire to, while being fondled by lobbyists. If we don't count and we don't care and we don't show up, then they can carry on business as usual. Now you tell me, does that sound like an enlightened democracy or a Banana Republic? Perhaps Lincoln was wrong and you can fool all of the people all of the time. We will see.

Without change, we are doomed to be a nation in decline. Without participation in our franchise, the vote, we are a threat to ourselves and everyone else. If we are the best humanity has to offer in government and we are so inept, what is the fate of us all? If our generation doesn't change things for the better, then who will?

When you vote in Los Angeles this election cycle, you get a colorful sticker to wear that proudly proclaims, "Make A Difference – 1 Vote Counts." Not yet. If we are the last best chance for humanity, then we better get to work or learn to speak another language so we can communicate with our new bosses, who will gladly set up shop right here in the Banana Republic of the United States of America.

The Highway To Hell

September 2005

They say that the highway to hell is paved with good intentions. Well, guess what, the same road can be constructed for even less and at a much faster rate by people with bad, very bad intentions. Even if the mounting "biblical" tragedy of the Deep South is attributed to "benign neglect", as most politicians of both parties with their fingers in the pie and the levee would have you believe, I can assure you that the neglect was anything but "benign". And the intentions were anything but good.

Despair

I am haunted by nightmares of things that I have not seen. In the bowels of the great public edifices of New Orleans, unspeakable acts of horror were played out night after night. As the help that never was grew more distant, the darkness that fell at night began to fall all day and consumed more and more of the guilty and the innocent. In our deep revulsion, we can only pray that the victims in those crucibles of malevolence didn't suffer as much as we know they did. And in our anger, even a non-violent person can only hope that the retribution for those who committed the crimes is more than sufficient. However, while we do know who the victims are, mostly by their classification as "living in poverty," the identity of the criminals is just coming to light. The hell so aptly reported by the suddenly awakened press had its' origins long ago, many years before the ill winds that blew in with September 2005. What evil was lurking in the hearts of those who refused to provide for the protection of the people of New Orleans, let alone the opportunity to rise above their circumstance? Obviously, it was the evil of indifference and self-interest. Every level of government failed the people left behind. It failed them over the many decades it took to imprison them in the grinding poverty of the America that lives in the shadows. Katrina, the perfect storm, only lifted the veil so all the world could see America as it truly is; two Americas, one for the haves and one for the "never gonna haves." Condemnation will be swift for the perpetrators of the heinous acts roiling with the stench in the condemned New Orleans of the past week but when will the masters of deceit, who concocted the gumbo of despair, be brought to justice?

Hope

Amidst the hurly-burly pace of the sunset of civility that gripped New Orleans in the wake of the perfect storm, there arose a mighty testament to the better angels of our nature. The obvious angels that acted without waiting to ask for permission were the doctors, nurses, helicopter pilots, EMT workers, police, firefighters, reporters (yes, at last the reporters!) and their crews, and so many more compassionate and selfless giants of charity, who stayed to help or arrived to help as well as those who have come since. But if you want to know whom the heroes and heroines of New Orleans are - watch those images of the true saints who came marching in. See the faces of the good people of New Orleans. There they are. Stripped of all that they knew or owned, however meager it may have been. Denied the much bally-hooed and seldom delivered American Dream, let alone rescue. Stranded on the highway overpasses and at the Super Dome and the Convention Center and in the roads and in the water and on the rooftops waving their signs. Oh, what a mighty host of angels. How many of these unfortunate souls endured this without resorting to the looting and raping and murdering so widely reported? The answer is, almost all of them.

With their dignity intact, these pillars of civic courage and deportment waited for their government to do the right thing. They did not riot. They did not lose their humanity. They showed the world what the human spirit is capable of. In this gut-wrenching scene of apocalyptic destruction, they walked tall. When has there ever been a nobler group of Americans? The lowest of the low showed the world that they are in fact, not at the bottom of society but are the best that America has to offer. We owe them far too much to ever be repaid. What could ever compensate them for the tragedy of their existence before and after Katrina? These are the famous Saints of New Orleans, we have heard lauded so many times in song. To them, their staunch civility and to those who did come to their rescue without permission or direction, we must all bow deeply. They held their heads up and they kept hope alive, theirs and ours.

Action

Amidst all that we will do to rebuild this shattered piece of America, there is another task at hand. We must gird ourselves for the oozing filth of evasion, equivocation and rationalization that will pour over us from our elected officials. Be aware, the finger pointing is only designed to deflect guilt and responsibility. But we know who is responsible. We know who is guilty. We know whom to blame. Every damn one of them who ever voted for any of the heinous money-grabbing schemes that have robbed us, the citizens, of our hard earned place in the sun. Every one of them who lined their pockets with our hard earned taxes. Every one of them who is planning as you read this to fleece us of our heritage (i.e. the very land, water and air of this nation and the world). Every one of them who would sell their own family down the sewer for another re-election. Every one of them who is addicted to the glow of the gold poured down their throats by the corrupt corporations who are out to control everything. They are the worst criminals in this sad display of so-called "benign neglect." When will they be brought to justice?

So, to them, the arch criminals, let us all make a solemn pledge. We will take a look at every vote you have cast. We will see where in your votes you put your interests and those of the lobbyists before the citizens. We will pay attention to what you are saying and doing. We will question your conclusions. We will make you earn our vote. We will hold you accountable for this disaster and all others like the Debacle in Iraq. We will stay on your case. We will not fall asleep and let you drive us down the "Highway To Hell." And most importantly, we will begin with our own party, the Democratic Party of the United States of America. When Bill Clinton said he was going to get rid of "welfare as we know it", he began the great sellout of the FDR America, of the Democratic Party. Down the slope we fell, right into the arms of the true evildoers. They are dismantling our America, piece by piece. And they are doing it with the help of far too many Democrats.

It's time to clean our own house. Wake up and stay awake. Join every possible official body of the Democratic Party you can and let us honor the good citizens of New Orleans and Biloxi and Gulf Port and all of the other devastated cities of "our" country by forming a more perfect union and responsible Party. Let us begin that process by forming a Democratic Party with the compassion of Jimmy Carter, the courage of FDR, the straight talk of Harry Truman and the vision of JFK. Let us reject the DLC and all those who hide in the corporate shadows and deny the fact that we are no better than how we treat the most vulnerable among us.

We have much to do. Katrina has blown over but the real storm is just now rising. Remember those faces. Remember what we found out. Remember, New Orleans and all the rest of us have been sold down the river but we know how to swim and float and help each other keep going "'til we get to a better place." And most importantly, remember, we can change this. We will change this, one vote, one life and one day at a time. Banish your despair and nurture your hope. Then ACT !!!!!!!!

Building The People's House

June 2006

Tom Hayden's analysis of the recent primary election was spot on. In it, he laid out the scenario surrounding the Marcy Winograd campaign for Congress, in the 36th CD. Winograd's courage in taking on the CDP infrastructure, Limousine Liberals and those pious electeds who portray themselves as Progressives and act as incumbents, was a defining moment for all Progressive Liberal Democratic grassroots activists in California and across the nation. Harman's sudden left turn, on Iraq, NSA spying and the Patriot Act, was well worth the effort.

As important as Marcy's campaign was to all of us, there were other notable races across the state. DLC so-called Moderates, bullied along by Rahm Emanuel and Chuck Schumer, lost two important races to Progressive Democrats. Cynthia Matthews bested Russ Warner in the 26th and Jerry McNerney outpolled Steve Filson in the 11th. Probably the most heartening Progressive victory was Deborah Bowen's win over Deborah Ortiz, the DLC chosen candidate, for Secretary of State.

The implications of a Bowen victory, in the general election this November against Republican Bruce McPherson, will reverberate across the country because Bowen is the strongest Election Integrity advocate running for statewide office in California.

In all of these races, DLC Establishment Democrat money and strong-arm tactics could not defeat highly motivated true grassroots Progressive communities. In contrast, Busby's race, against Bibray, in the 50th CD, proved once again that a DLC so-called Moderate candidate still couldn't beat an RNC division, fear and intolerance candidate.

In Humboldt County, voters passed Measure T, which says that corporations do not have the same rights as persons, when participating in political campaigns. That law will end in up in court and go all the way to the Supremes. In my Los Angeles 42nd AD County Central Committee race, I lost, along with all of the other Progressives, to an incumbents only sweep. Next door in the 41st, all of the Progressives won. That certainly shows us, where the Establishment is and isn't hanging on to power.

We learned a lot in this election cycle, especially about the condition of the California Democratic Party and the Progressive Movement. Our movement is built on analysis and then action. My analysis of the June 2006 election is as follows:

Incumbency, Endorsement and Corporate/Big Donor Money are the tools of the DLC Establishment machine.

In most cases, from Central Committee to Presidential elections, the Clinton/DLC wing of the Party still holds the line against the growing Progressive Movement. They are so seductive, that Electeds, Celebrities and Pundits eagerly fall under their sway. They are so persuasive, that the Democratic rank and file remains 65% to 35% under their thumb and willingly so.

In far too many cases, endorsement in the primary season is another means of enforcement to maintain the status quo and payback or create favors. It needs to be reformed or abolished. It creates an over-heated atmosphere where friends are at odds and principle is too easily maligned or traded for short-term gain or long-term profit. Policy debate is drowned in a swamp of personality polishing. Voters stayed away from the polls in droves, thereby registering the lack of persuasion of the much-prized endorsements. The Sierra Club, Barbara Lee, Barbara Boxer and Maxine Waters endorsing Harman and not Winograd, are the most glaring examples of the ludicrous nature of the current endorsement system.

Perhaps, it is just primal human nature that makes us so anxious to trade principle for profit. Maybe, it's greed or fear or that need to be loved, that motivates the resistance to change and the victory of narrow over enlightened self-interest. No matter, change is inevitable and the potential for the greater good is alive and well. The Progressive Movement, inside and outside of the Democratic Party, is that change and that potential, today. Lincoln's better angels of our nature are as powerful as the forces arrayed against them but require more diligence to be realized. I offer the following actions to realize our potential and achieve our goals:

To overcome our shortcomings and bolster our resolve, we must better organize ourselves as a movement. This requires planning and the transformation of vertical personal ambition into horizontal community ambition, E Pluribus Unum.

In order to transform the CDP, we need to elect Progressives to at least 16% more of the delegate seats in the CDP Central Committee Assembly District elections of January 2007. That would create a 51% Progressive majority. Better still would be to have super majority of over 60% in total. We need to enact Clean Money Campaign Financing, at every level of governance. We must continue to pressure every jurisdiction, to insure Secure Voting Procedures so that every vote is counted as cast. We need to grow the Progressive Movement, especially in the Assembly Districts where the Incumbents -Only dictum prevails.

We need to create a National Progressive Coalition

All of the National Progressive Organizations plus the State Democratic Party Progressive Caucuses should coordinate together on strategy and tactics. That coalition must give up the narrow interests of the leadership of each group in favor of the broad interests of all groups and learn to work together for the Common Good.

Most importantly, we must never give into the weakness of despair but must promote the strength of hope. We have already made a great difference in the destiny of the nation and humanity and we can do much more. We must create within ourselves and within the Progressive Movement a thousand citizens of courage like Marcy Winograd. Our thanks go out to every citizen like Marcy, who stood up, showed up and spoke up. This has been a good beginning. Now, it is back to work building the people's house.

President Joe Lieberman:
Deal or No Deal?

November 2006

Well my friends, we certainly find ourselves on the horns of a dilemma, don't we? We're here in the store and we want to buy the blue dress but we need to buy the grey suit and we only have enough money for one item. The blue dress would be more satisfying emotionally but the grey suit would last longer and be more practical. What to do?

I am so anxious to make every member of BushCo and the Republican Anarchy Collective do the perp walk that I'm tingling all over. Talk about a Christmas present! But wait; what if it all comes true? Let's play that scenario out. For our guides, let us all study the Nixon Impeachment (not that bogus Clinton affair), the 25th Amendment and the Presidential Succession Act of 1947.

Bush and Cheney are certainly guilty of committing "high crimes and misdemeanors" along with a colorful assortment of prosecutable felonies. On this we all can agree. They both should be brought before an international court for crimes against humanity. (While we're at it let's make sure we pick up Henry Kissinger on the way there). Once more we can find consensus. So, let the impeachments begin!

Now, many have suggested that both Dick & W should be impeached together, you know, clean sweep and all. Sorry, the Supreme Court probably wouldn't allow that since it would deprive them of due process. Only one trial in the Senate at a time would be fair or practical. We could spend a year or so fighting that out in the courts, which we would, because there is no provision for two trials at once, whereas there is for one. So, we decide to impeach W. Wait a minute - that makes Dick the Pres. Not acceptable. So, let's try Dick first. OK, let's say we get the necessary articles of impeachment in the house and we successfully impeach the Veep in the Senate. Whew, that only took 6 to 12 months.

Now, W appoints a new Veep – read the 25th Amendment. Who would George ll appoint? Well, he won't appoint a Republican because the new Democratic Congress would not ratify it. So, he'd have to appoint a Democrat. Run the list of Democrats across your fevered brow and tell me who would accept this appointment? Also, which Democrat would be acceptable to the Republicans – they will be needed in this process after all.

All right, it won't be anyone who is contemplating a run for the White House. Remember what happened to Gerald Ford? It will be a so-called moderate, so as not to inflame the wings of this turkey. Who can it be now? Hmm… Yes, you are right. We have a winner! Meet the new Vice President. Jiltin' Joe Lieberman - darling of the disgruntled Republican - master of the muddled middle DLC Dems. Now we impeach the Shrub at 1600 Pennsylvania Avenue and voila – President Joe Lieberman.

Thank goodness that entire process from investigations to swearing in only took up the entire two years before the next Presidential election, which of course Joe will be running in as the sitting "Democratic" President. Now, we can get back to the business of the people, eliminating poverty, lowering the cost of prescription drugs, rolling back the environmental degradation of the past twelve years, rebuilding New Orleans, investigating the skullduggery of the Executive branch, repealing the curbs to our civil rights and most importantly getting out of Iraq.

You see - the dream can turn into a nightmare. Which one of the vital issues I just mentioned would you sacrifice to impeach these heinous buffoons? How much more time would you spend in Iraq while we attempt to do so? How many poverty level wage earners would you deny even a paltry minimum wage raise to, while the proceedings drag on? A dilemma is by definition, "a situation requiring a choice between equally undesirable alternatives." If we do the work, which needs desperately to be done, we must leave the culprits in office, neutered and willing to sign our legislation to save their Party and their legacy. If we attack and win, which we are morally correct in doing, we lose the legislation and the perp walk for the underlings plus Jiltin' Joe and DLC rise to recapture the DNC and fracture the Progressive Movement for years to come.

If you don't think it could happen - think again. Study your Constitution. Do the historical analysis. I have and find myself in complete agreement with the plans of the Speaker-elect. I support Nancy Pelosi's strategy and tactics. I encourage you to do the same.

Independence Day 2007

July 2007

Americans near and far: July 4th is the day to remember the founding of our Republic. Even if it is not the actual date of the signing of the Declaration of Independence (July 2nd), it is the day of the vote of adoption by the colonies, publication of the document and thus the day of celebration beginning in 1777. Two hundred and thirty years later, our nation is staggering under the oppression of a tyrant named George once again. His impudent band of lawless henchmen have proven to be an ironic and feckless foil to the other son of oil – Osama Bin Laden - and his equally anarchistic gang of killers and thugs. Both groups are bent on the destruction of the Western Ideal as enshrined in our Declaration of 1776 – one from within and one from without.

So, we have come this far only to be confronted by the same mendacity of greed and delusional sanctimonious violence that the Founders revolted against. Jefferson, who was the principal author of the Declaration, also remarked that the "price of freedom is eternal vigilance." Bush, Cheney and Bin Laden are stark reminders of the price of our freedom, our independence. Let us confront them together in the spirit of the Founders that ennobled the American cause. Let us band together in the spirit of the original motto of E Pluribus Unum. Let us restore our purpose stated so eloquently in that Declaration - that "we mutually pledge to each other our Lives, our fortunes and our sacred Honor."

When you watch the fireworks on the 4th, take the time to remember those who are in harm's way, both American and all other citizens of the world. Then, let's get to work and change the course of the state, the nation and the globe. Now is the time. This is the place and "We are the People!"

Rove and the Rubes

September 2007

When I was growing up in the rural heartland of America and the almost vacant Far West during the 50's and early 60's, there were two traveling shows that came to town each year. Both pitched tents and invited the rubes in. One was the circus. The other was the preacher. Circus performers played to our childish romance with the strange world around us and made you laugh and gasp with awe at things you didn't see every day walking down Main Street. Preachers played to our fears of things we could not see and the life beyond death. And so it was, that when Karl Rove, Karen Hughes and Shrub came rumbling into town looking like a circus, I knew which tent was being pitched. Now, it seems that most Americans are catching on as well.

Not unlike Elmer Gantry, Karl has manipulated the earnest dry-drunk Preacher while hiding in the shadows. Karl has proven to be a master craftsman of smoke and mirrors and "boy howdy have the rubes bought it." Alas, every show knows when it's time to move on except for the one's that come to believe that their illusion is in fact, reality. So it is with Karl. Desperate to conjure his veil of fear once again, he became so impatient with the headliner after dwindling ticket sales that he shoved him off the stage. From behind the curtain, he suddenly appeared to gin up the crowd with the final retribution of the God-less demons stealing our very own souls.

Some people are justifiably frightened of what Karl can do but I am not. His snickering implication of Liberal treason is falling on deaf ears. The Neo-Con tyranny is crumbling around him. The Downing Street memo has proven what we all knew, those of us who had caught his type of act before. Yes, the rubes bought it for a while but after enough of their daughters and sons, mothers and fathers, brothers and sisters had perished in the desert even they have had enough. Frightened Democrats who were hiding in the tent and some Republicans who read the bad reviews are denying they ever attended the show. They all claim to have been snookered by the velvet-tongued crew from Texas and the PNAC think tank boys. When the facts of the rigged elections and war for profits sideshows are finally revealed, no one will claim to have ever known Karl Rove, let alone agreed with him. Just like Joe McCarthy and Richard Nixon before him, his path of destruction will have consumed many but ultimately it will end and he will be in tatters; slinking out of town, with the gabbing talking heads who have run out of ears for their fire and brimstone.

Like many of us here in Hollywood, I took my feelings of not fitting in and ran away with the circus. We were outsiders who banded together to form a more beautiful world of fantasy and romance. It's an honest business, show business. We know it's fake and you should too. It's the people who felt left out over in that other tent you have to keep an eye on. There will be other Karl Roves; same show, different name. As long as they're not whipping the crowd into frenzy to do awful things, they're OK. When they come after the non-believers with vengeance in their eyes, it's time to prepare yourself for a long night of trouble.

Maybe in the end Karl Rove with his reign of terror and fear mongering will have done something of value for America? Maybe the final result of this vile and duplicitous man and his retribution against the do-gooders will be a reawakening of the Liberal, Progressive and Democratic citizens who spent too many years basking in their achievements and chasing fame and fortune. Maybe us rubes will be better off because we suffered the terrible years of Karl Rove. I think we will.

Truth and the War

May 2008

- There were no weapons of Mass Destruction left in Iraq

- There was no Al Queda in Iraq

- There was no danger of a mushroom cloud from Iraq

- There was no purchase of Yellow Cake uranium from Niger by Iraq

- The President, Vice-president, Secretary of State, head of the CIA and much of the Executive lied about all of this as a pretext to wage war in Iraq

- The Vice President and the WH COS Karl Rove outed Valerie Plame thus committing an act of treason

- The Patriot Act and Illegal Wiretapping were not legal or necessary to insure our security and have robbed us of our liberty

- There were and are many High Crimes and Misdemeanors that were committed by the Executive up to the Top

- Congress has abdicated its duty to the American Public and its oath to defend the

Constitution by not stopping the War and Impeaching the President and Vice President

- Democrats up to the Top in the Congress have been complicit in this dereliction of duty in the name of National Security

- Pragmatism, not enough votes and we can't be seen as not supporting the troops are the hollow reasons given by the current Democratic Party leadership for support of these continuing crimes and the War

- The American public has lost faith in both the Congress and the Executive with the lowest approval ratings in history

Congress is finally moving to shut one of the more egregious forms of Iraq war profiteering: defense contractors using offshore shell companies to avoid paying their fair share of payroll taxes. No one will be surprised to hear that one of the suspected prime offenders is KBR, the Texas-based defense contractor, formerly a part of the Halliburton conglomerate allied with Vice President Dick Cheney. According to a report in The Boston Globe, KBR, which has landed billions in Iraq contracts, has used two Cayman shell companies to avoid paying hundreds of millions in payroll, Medicare and unemployment taxes. Unfortunately right now there is nothing illegal about this.

Listen to this letter from a member of my Democratic club:

Sam's Letter -

Here's what gets me steamed. The Iraq War is being paid for with money borrowed from foreign countries. We then have to pay them back with interest. This is the first time since the Revolutionary War this has EVER happened (smell that fishy odor?). And the wealthiest elite aren't being taxed more (as in every other past war) but had their taxes CUT! But if you think that is bad, read below! Please note. The company that is dodging taxes WHILE TAKING OUR TAX MONEY is KBR, a company formerly a part of Dick Cheney's Halliburton. Another thing I HATE HATE HATE about this war is how all the people involved in starting it are making billions off of it! And if you question them, they claim you are being unpatriotic and "How dare you threaten our troops by being disloyal and questioning a defense contractor!" Man, these people are the wickedest of the wicked! We have military men and women dying and getting maimed and screwing up their minds and these companies are shortening them in taxes while making a profit!

Sam Park
Valley Democrats United Board

Legacy of Truth

In war, truth is the first casualty.

~ Aeschylus

All wars are fought for money.

~ Socrates

The worst crimes were dared by a few, willed by more and tolerated by all.

~ Tacitus

General Truths

It is only those who have neither fired a shot nor heard the shrieks and groans of the wounded who cry aloud for blood...War is hell.

~ General William Tecumseh Sherman

War is a racket. It always has been. It is possibly the oldest, easily the most profitable, surely the most vicious.

~ General Smedley Butler

Presidential Truths

Great is the guilt of an unnecessary war.

~ John Adams

If Tyranny and Oppression come to this land, it will be in the guise of fighting a foreign enemy.

~ **James Madison**

Behind the ostensible government sits enthroned an invisible government owing no allegiance and acknowledging no responsibility to the people.

~ **Theodore Roosevelt**

Preventive war was an invention of Hitler. Frankly, I would not even listen to anyone seriously that came and talked about such a thing.

~ **Dwight D. Eisenhower**

Military glory--that attractive rainbow that rises in showers of blood--that serpent's eye that charms to destroy...

~ **Abraham Lincoln**

American Truths

No matter that patriotism is too often the refuge of scoundrels. Dissent, rebellion, and all-around hell raising remain the true duty of patriots.

~ **Barbara Ehrenreich**

You're not supposed to be so blind with patriotism that you can't face reality. Wrong is wrong no matter who does it or who says it.

~ **Malcolm X**

I love America more than any other country in the world and, exactly for this reason, I insist on the right to criticize her perpetually.

~ James Baldwin

The greatest purveyor of violence in the world today is my own government.

~ Dr. Martin Luther King Jr.

To some degree it matters who's in office, but it matters more how much pressure they're under from the public.

~ Noam Chomsky

The Department of Defense is the behemoth...With an annual budget larger than the gross domestic product of Russia, it is an empire.

~The 9/11 Commission Report

The Central Intelligence Agency owns everyone of any significance in the major media.

~ William Colby, former CIA director

World Truths

The tyranny of a prince in an oligarchy is not so dangerous to public welfare as the apathy of a citizen in a democracy.

~ Montesquieu

Truth stands, even if there be no public support. It is self-sustained.

~ **Mahatma Gandhi**

What a country calls its vital... interests are not things that help its people live, but things that help it make war.

~ **Simone Weil**

A state of war only serves as an excuse for domestic tyranny.

~ **Aleksandr Solzhenitsyn**
Lies, Delusions and Tyranny

It's not a matter of what is true that counts but a matter of what is perceived to be true.

~ **Henry Kissinger**

I just want you to know that, when we talk about war, we're really talking about peace.

~ **George W. Bush**

Evil men, obsessed with ambition and unburdened by conscience, must be taken very seriously--and we must stop them before their crimes can multiply.

~ **George W. Bush**

Death has a tendency to encourage a depressing view of war.

~ Donald Rumsfeld

There are a lot of people who lie and get away with it, and that's just a fact.

~ Donald Rumsfeld

Why should we hear about body bags, and deaths...I mean, it's not relevant. So why should I waste my beautiful mind on something like that?

~ Barbara Bush

*(Remarks delivered at a
Los Angeles County Democratic Party Forum ~
Summer 2008)*

PART VI

Dems in D'Town
August 2008

Walkin' the Planks:
The DNC Platform Metamorphosis

August 2008

Peruse the following excerpts from the platform and policy positions of a state Democratic Party, presumptive nominee and the national committee and you will notice a thread of unremarkable but substantial importance: the movement from left to right in the process of drafting a national platform for the DNC.

When I quizzed the staff at the DNC, who were tasked with writing the draft platform language in its final form, they informed me that the main policy points were from Obama's positions online. These were then modified by the subsequent hearings this past month. Many progressive Democrats had told me this was not the case. So, I did some research to see what was in fact the truth of the process.

First, progressive platform language, from state Democratic Party platforms and informal house meetings held around the nation, was rejected or marginalized at these hearings. Next, it appears that the liberal language of the Obama website was then watered down into the nominal conservative language that we are poised to vote on at the Denver convention. What was up? Who was promoting this meandering swoon? I believe the reason for this surge from left to right, from progressive to liberal to conservative is obvious -

the DLC and corporate Cronies are still in control of the Democratic Party apparatus.

Rather than drone on about this observation - and chilling reality - I have provided a brief overview of three platforms: the California Democratic Party 2008 platform, the Barack Obama policy positions and the DNC draft platform planks on the Internet, communications, media and free speech. At the end of this post, I have also included excerpts from each of those papers for those who want to see the actual language. Read these excerpts carefully and you will divine the invisible hand of Crony at work.

In California, the largest state Democratic Party, we drafted and passed a communications and media plank, centered on the Internet that provides a positive progressive and labor stance for all communications in America. This was one of the outcomes of the CDP Labor and Progressive caucuses working successfully together on a Net Neutrality resolution the year before and years of lobbying the CDP Platform committee for progressive language. I am a coauthor of both the resolution and the plank. Central to this plank is maintaining the Internet as a public utility, diversity of media ownership and protection against violations of the law, especially our First Amendment rights, by either the government or business interests. This is what a progressive platform plank should support and look like.

Now look at the Internet and media positions espoused by Barack Obama on his website. They come from a principled liberal candidate but fall short of progressive positions. Although strong on many points, they do not mention maintaining the Internet as a public utility. Even while calling for diversity of ownership, they refrain from explicit language affirming the citizen's eminent domain over this new and vitally important communications media. Then, they spend some time mentioning the protection of children from Internet crime - laudable but not paramount.

Finally, we have the proposed media DNC Platform plank, to be ratified in Denver. In the mushy feel good language of the rest of the platform, they invoke the spirit of openness but fail to mention the distinction between public and private ownership of the Internet. They never mention diversity of media ownership. They devote almost half of the plank to protecting children from online crime, which though relevant is not the most pressing issue regarding media in America. While extolling broadband rollout for rural America they fail to include the same provisions for underserved or poor Americans. Their privacy language is vague and leaves out First Amendment guarantees. This plank is a microcosm of the macro platform and reveals the "change" from left to right, citizens to corporations, in stark terms. There is a reason for this metamorphosis - you guessed it - the DLC.

DLC consultants have always maintained that working class Americans will reject progressive policy that is specific and meaningful. They consistently recommend the "stand for nothing principle" as the best way to get candidates elected. Just when the public is clamoring for change they can believe in, the DLC ludicrously insists on the status quo. It is all a dodge and the last 16 years of election cycles prove its inefficacy.

Working class Americans are the artifice used by the DLC to promote Crony politics, government and business. That should come as no surprise to those who know that the DLC is a wholly owned subsidiary of Crony corporate interests. Look at the private parties and elite events scheduled for Denver and you can see the platform that the DLC, firmly in control of the Democratic Party, stands on: whoever has the gold - makes the rules.

We must change this paradigm. Progressive policy is the way out of the swamp of the DLC Crony past. Apparently that memo has yet to reach the DNC Platform committee. Someone needs to make sure that Barack Obama gets it.

Platform and policy excerpts:

Internet, Free Speech and Communications: (from the California Democratic Party Platform 2008)

California Democrats, in order to promote vigorous free speech, a vibrant business community, and unfettered access to all information on the Internet, support policies to preserve an open, neutral and interconnected Internet. California Democrats strongly agree with recent rulings by the Federal Election Commission that political communications, including blogging, which take place independent of a political party, committee or candidate, receive a media exemption from campaign finance regulations. California Democrats further reaffirm their support of the right to free speech as expressed in the First Amendment, including the right to critique any elected official or comment on any and all public policy, whether during war or peace, without fear of reprisal.

To promote and support the Internet, Free Speech and Communications California Democrats will:

• Support protections against any degradation or blocking of access to any websites or content on the Internet to which access is legal and guaranteed by the Constitution;

• Insure that consumers have the right to free email and that any and all communications will be protected from warrantless search and seizure as guaranteed in the Constitution;

• Encourage build-out of high speed networks to all homes and businesses so that everyone, especially rural and underserved areas, can access content of their choice and upload or download what they want on the Internet as a public utility maintained by union workers;

• Establish and secure ownership limits on private sector mass media to encourage and provide more cultural diversity, while protecting the openness, accessibility and integrity of the Internet as a public media resource for all Americans, regardless of income.

Barack Obama's Plan: (from his website)

Ensure the Full and Free Exchange of Information through an Open Internet and Diverse Media Outlets

Protect the Openness of the Internet: A key reason the Internet has been such a success is because it is the most open network in history. It needs to stay that way. Barack Obama strongly supports the principle of network neutrality to preserve the benefits of open competition on the Internet. Users must be free to access content, to use applications, and to attach personal devices. They have a right to receive accurate and honest information about service plans. But these guarantees are not enough to prevent network providers from discriminating in ways that limit the freedom of expression on the Internet. Because most Americans only have a choice of only one or two broadband carriers, carriers are tempted to impose a toll charge on content and services, discriminating against websites that are unwilling to pay for equal treatment. This could create a two-tier Internet in which websites with the best relationships with network providers can get the fastest access to consumers, while all competing websites remain in a slower lane. Such a result would threaten innovation, the open tradition and architecture of the Internet, and competition among content and backbone providers. It would also threaten the equality of speech through which the Internet has begun to transform American political and cultural discourse. Barack Obama supports the basic principle that network providers should not be allowed to charge fees to privilege the content or applications of some web sites and Internet applications over others. This principle will ensure that the new competitors, especially small or non-profit speakers, have the same opportunity as incumbents to innovate on the Internet and to reach large audiences. Obama will protect the Internet's traditional openness to innovation and creativity and ensure that it remains a platform for free speech and innovation that will benefit consumers and our democracy.

Encourage Diversity in Media Ownership: Barack Obama believes that the nation's rules ensuring diversity of media ownership are critical to the public interest. Unfortunately, over the past several years, the Federal Communications Commission has promoted the concept of consolidation over diversity. Barack Obama believes that providing opportunities for minority-owned businesses to own radio and television stations is fundamental to creating the diverse media environment that federal law requires and the country deserves and demands. As president, he will encourage diversity in the ownership of broadcast media, promote the development of new media outlets for expression of diverse viewpoints, and clarify the public interest obligations of broadcasters who occupy the nation's spectrum. An Obama presidency will promote greater coverage of local issues and better responsiveness by broadcasters to the communities they serve.

Protect Our Children While Preserving the First Amendment: By making information freely available from untold numbers of sources, the

Internet and more traditional media outlets have a huge influence on our children.

A Connected America (from the DNC Platform Committee DRAFT – 08/07/08)

In the 21st century, our world is more intertwined than at any time in human history. This new connectedness presents us with untold opportunities for innovation, but also new challenges. We will protect the Internet's traditional openness to innovation and creativity and ensure that it remains a dynamic platform for free speech, innovation, and creativity. We will implement a national broadband strategy, especially in rural areas, that enables every American household, school, library and hospital to connect to a world-class communications infrastructure. We will rededicate our nation to ensuring that all Americans have access to broadband and the skills to use it effectively. In an increasingly technology-rich, knowledge-based economy, connectivity is a key part of the solution to many of our most important challenges: job creation, economic growth, energy, health care, and education. We will establish a Chief Technology Officer for the nation, to ensure we use technology to enhance the functioning, transparency, and expertise of government, including establishing a national interoperable public safety communications network to help first responders at the local, state and national level communicate with one another during a crisis.

We will toughen penalties, increase enforcement resources, and spur private sector cooperation with law enforcement to identify and prosecute those who exploit the Internet to try to harm children. We will encourage more educational content on the Web and in our media. We will give parents the tools and information they need to manage (in ways fully consistent with the First Amendment) what their children see on television and the Internet. We will strengthen privacy protections in the digital age and will harness the power of technology to hold government and business accountable for violations of personal privacy.

(This article was published on the Huffington Post under the title of, "Business-Friendly Democratic party Platform Reflects Interests of Party Leaders" – September 2008)

Yellow Doggin' It in D'Town

August 2008

Thunderheads roiled the Rockies surrounding D'Town. Surging through the 16th Street mall came the massed and masked desperadoes, demanding an end to the war and the empire. Closely watched and nervously corralled by every conceivable form of police and paramilitary squad on the alert for reported low tech weapons of mass destruction – round and round the downtown of Denver they swirled. The Democrats were swarming in Denver. And then there were the delegates.

High above the streets, the irked Clinton compatriots were conjuring one last stand for the vanishing dream of insurrection. Obama had not arrived but was ever present, visibly iconic - on buttons, posters, banners, tickets and more. Bigwigs, high rollers and grand poobahs of every style, strut and station floated above it all.

That's what this observer witnessed in just the first few hours of the Democratic Convention on Sunday. Tension is palpable among the delegates as everyone wonders what the Clinton delegates are going to do in the coming days. As one of those delegates, a Progressive Democrat no less, I recommend that we all get behind the nominee. Progressives are rallying to Obama's candidacy and with good reason – he is all that lies between the Republic and McCain.

At the Progressive Democrats of America's Progressive Central meeting, Tom Hayden, Rep. Barbara Lee, Norman Solomon, Jim Hightower and every speaker urged support for Obama's election if not his policy positions. As Paul Krugman has remarked – *the difference between Barack Obama and Bill Clinton is us* – the Progressive Movement. Can we elect a centrist and then turn him progressive? I think we can.

It is all achingly historic and terrifying at once. Hope for change, balanced with the recent history of electoral theft, imbues the proceedings. Will every citizen on the left of the political spectrum coalesce behind this candidate? This Party? Corrupted by Crony campaign contributions and the incessant compliant search for more of them? Do you dare to dream? I do.

We are off on a Dr. Suessian cavort - a frolicking, rollicking romp. A deadly serious, fanfoozeling, bamboozolous, ratatatootaling raucous ride down the rapids of dissent, consent and hopefully - consensus.

(This article was published on the Huffington Post under the title of, "A Yellow Dog Delegate in D'Town" – August 2008)

The Mothership Hovers Above D'Town:
Close Encounters With Progressive Policy

August 2008

Beneath a massive prop that resembled nothing as much as it did the "Mothership" from "Close Encounters of the Third Kind," strode the stars for the first scene of the 2008 Democratic Convention. Down the gangway they strolled, to a strong R&B beat and a tightly scripted teleprompter. As they read their carefully scrubbed lines, they were bathed in an ethereal light show from above and beyond. It was a triumph of lighting, stagecraft, good intentions and empty calories.

Strangely, there was precious little sauce on the Q at this festive soul session. It was as if the entire endeavor had been focus-grouped to death. Madmen had dumbed it down. Sizzle it did but steak it was not. Not for lack of good intentions did this extravaganza fall flat though. No – everyone meant well but as Shakespeare wrote, "many a slip twixt cup and lip."

What was missing in this mélange of Madison Avenue sure fire branding, I wondered as the hours crept by? Then it struck me – with everyone reading from a script you need very good writers to keep the audience's attention. To have a truly transformative evening in the theater, you need words that are authentic and not "one size fits all." This isn't McDonald's; this is people's fate we are talking about. We were consuming the bones of the Liberal ideal with the marrow sucked out of them. Crony was in the house.

It is fair to say that none of the players in our drama were to blame. On the contrary, they all did their bits in earnest. However, only one spoke the truth that hid behind the intent of the coming election. America wants rid of its Republican abusers and Rep. Jim Leach, a Republican no less, delivered the stinging rebuke as if possessed by the ghost of liberal Republicans of days gone by. Then, sheer will lifted Ted Kennedy on to the stage and his emotional delivery invoked the liberal ghosts of Democratic days gone by. These were highlights of the evening for policy purveyance and good old-fashioned rabble rousing. Whenever the conversation turned to economics though, as it often did, they rolled out the mush.

Democrats have an Achilles heal when they speak of the economy. Democrats always portray their constituents as victims. Some wise-guy admeister or Beltway consulting group seems to have convinced Democrats long ago that pathos is the way to the voter's hearts. I disagree. Why is it necessary to summon moral clarity only through pity? Not one Democratic policy position needs a dour tone to succeed.

In economics for instance, why not employ the positive methods and progressive economic policy Mark Pash explores on his new website, www.economicsfordemocrats.com? I was so impressed with his concepts I collaborated with him on the essays. He says it simply and with vigor – progressive economics will make more money for everyone than conservative or moderate economics. Nothing mushy about that statement. He has done a thorough analysis to back it up as well. So, why not portray the poor, working poor and middle class as the bedrock of American business? After all, they do the work that makes the goods and services that pay the taxes and generate the sales. Democrats need to come from a place of strength not weakness. The subtext of every economic proposal tonight was let's be the good Party and help the victims. Ugh – that is not necessary.

Perhaps most poignantly missing from the evening was one iconic image, just one. On an evening that rightly exulted women, mothers and motherhood, the steadfast and tough-minded tenderness we all rely on, there was a mother missing. Amidst the glow of Nancy Pelosi's ascension to Speaker of the house, Rosalyn Carter's quiet fortitude, Caroline Kennedy's call to the courage of her father echoed in Barack Obama, Senator Claire McCaskill's pride of family, Marian Robinson's pride in her girl and Michelle Obama's pride in her two girls, there was someone's face oddly missing. Stanley Ann Dunham Soetoro's name was invoked but her eyes were not seen. She hovered above the proceedings as if she was a mystical apparition, unseen but deeply felt.

S. Ann Soetoro is Barack Obama's mother. She died at too early of an age but left a son of remarkable possibilities. We could have used a look into her eyes when her daughter, Barack's sister Maya Soetoro-Ng, called out her name.

Instead, we were left to imagine the reality of her life, her soul. She was there I suspect. The "Mothership" hovered but did not land.

Act one saw the distant promise of change without the clarity of positive progressive policy and action, the continued fear of losing that prevents the strength of taking a position or making a stand and the power of women without the prime woman. It was a close encounter on all counts and a good effort. It was close but no cigar.

(This article was published on the Huffington Post under the title of, "DNC Act One Failure: The One-Size-Fits-All Messaging" – August 2008)

Speak Up!

Sailing Around the Cape of Good Hope
With Hillary – finally…

August 2008

When last we saw Captain Clinton, she was traversing rough waters. Her crew was in full mutiny mode. Her first mate was on the bow, railing at the fickle seas and the cruel fates that had buffeted their ship of state for many a moon. The body politic languished in a discomposed mood, scrutinizing her every fidget to see if she would continue her quest for glory or tack back to safe harbor. On Tuesday evening, to a packed Democratic crowd at the Pepsi Center in D'Town, Senator Hillary Rodham Clinton revealed her schema. She was leaving the roiling deep behind and sailing around the Cape of Good Hope.

Not content with this outcome, ardent supporters of Senator Clinton scurried around the floor in the early hours of the conclave. They were attempting to gather enough signatures from the delegates to have her name put in nomination and voted on. It all came to naught. The die was cast. Senator Barack Obama will be the Democratic Party Presidential nominee.

Even as she spoke, I heard yells and bellows of mutiny here and there among the agitated crowd. These were underlined by furtive whispers discernable below the din of lasting approval and anguished realization. But bravely onward she went, charting a course for the future, Obama's future and ours.

We have all tasted defeat in our lives, maybe had our face rubbed in it occasionally but this was a humble pie of epic proportions. Yes, we know that she and her husband have had many of life's riches that will always be unavailable to the unwashed masses but here, before the world, their dream probably vanished for good and she was left to put on a brave face and pick up the pieces. Life with Bill Clinton has always seemed to track that way for Hillary. He cast a shadow for better and for worse across their tempestuous journey.

Who can say if perhaps on her own she would have risen to the heights of public service? Maybe she would have embraced progressive policy without the grand calculator by her side. Who knows?

Joylessly, she left that all behind, the possibilities, the promise and the precipitous plunge from the dream stage. Hillary did what she knew that she must do – she praised Obama and staked out her partnership with his dream. She endorsed him. Some say with faint praise. Others claimed unequivocally. No matter. The wheel of the Democratic Party is in other hands now, Senator Obama's hands. Spite, on the part of the Clinton Crew that aims at upending his Presidential bid, would come to haunt all of them. Mutiny, that immolates the fine thread of Democratic unity, would catapult the entire Republic, the globe, into the abyss of the Crony netherworld. What cold comfort could anyone derive from that?

I, like many of you, have harbored deep resentments for the pragmatic and unprincipled capitulation to corporate interests versus citizens interests that Hillary and Bill have far too often been a part of. Many of us have been vocal opponents of the DLC myth, of centrist supremacy in all things politic, that the Clintons have championed. However, I always considered them a worthy opponent and do not revel in their demise. You see, there but for fortune go you, go I.

As baby boomers and middle class children pulverized by the turbulent struggles of the Cold War era, any one of us could have set sail on their voyage. Don't kid yourself sailors, we are all more similar than we dare to admit.

As she leaves the big stage, she leaves with a modicum of dignity. She seemed to summon a part of her original delight in the liberal ideal and made some attempt to conjure it up. Somewhere in the depths of her ambition the flame still flickers. Too bad it never became a raging fire.

We should wish her well and keep the lighthouse on, for one day she may make port yet again, in the progressive movement that the young woman who became an avid advocate for children would have called home. Until then, she can console herself with the thought that sailing around the Cape of Good Hope is a damn sight better than braving the tortuous seas of Cape Horn.

Let us all, Progressives, Liberals, Democrats and Peaceniks, band together and send the entire Republican Party including the war-mongering Admiral McCain packing into that tempest. All hands on deck!

(This article was published on the Huffington Post under the title of, "Captain Hillary Sails' Round Good Hope At Last" – August 2008)

**Bill and Hill Get Back On The Porch
As Obama/Biden Get the Nod and Hawk Up!**

August 2008

At the 2008 Beijing Olympics, the Americans dropped a few baton handoffs in races they were expected to win. Today, the Clintons made sure that Obama got the handoff. Putting their considerable skills behind the newly minted Obama/Biden twofer, they slowly unfurled their acquiescence on their own terms, across D'Town, on Wednesday. Down South, they might say that the Big Blue Dogs got back up on the porch.

Giving up power is fraught with danger in most countries in the world. A transition that leaves the corpus intact is preferable but often just an ugly mashup. D'Town and the "D" Party have been teetering on the uncomfortable possibility of a civil war in the rank and file all week. Much to their credit, the Clintons passed the torch and with some of their uncanny panache.

First, Hillary assembled all of her delegates and released their votes, with the admonition that she was voting for Obama and if they were still with her they would as well. Grumbling perforated the low-key acceptance of the inevitable as gradually she brought them to her side, which is now Mr. O's side. Brother, they did not dig it but hey, Hill laid it down and they started to pick it up. That event was in the early afternoon. The Charmer from Hope capped it on the big stage later in the evening.

Rapturous applause greeted the fallen knight, as the remembrance of better days swelled in the concave. Bill reminded the sardine packed house that he was the man who took us to those better days. The assembly agreed. Even though the Telecommunications Act of 1996, NAFTA and a host of other Crony candy littered his reign, it was better times for most. Some moments it seemed as if Clinton was gritting his teeth at being muzzled by the Obama ordained script and then he would pivot ever so slightly and give his fans a taste of what he wanted to say anyway.

We all love a good entertainer and dear readers; Bill is as good as it gets on the political turf. It was kind of like an old time fun house ride in a carnival sideshow. There we were, knowing we were not going to get hurt but scared just enough to make it fun.

Frankly, the rest of the proceedings, other than the tightly staged roll call vote, meant to mollify the Clinton crew, were squeamishly militaristic. What is it with the Democrats and exhibitions of strength? Republicans want to bully the world. They have since World War ll. Russians love the bully game too, as do the Chinese, Indians and far too many other nations of patriarchal pugilists.

As our other fallen knight, John Edwards, rightly said, America must find something to be patriotic about other than war. Democrats need to find another way to say they are tough.

Well that won't happen soon, so, the hawks kept circling all night. We heard from generals, privates, veterans, Senators, cabinet members and heroic warriors of every description. On and on they droned about how Democrats are tough guys too. So what. Collaboration is the new paradigm, if the people on this planet are to survive. Combat is so played. Yeah, we will defend ourselves. As the only nation to have ever used nuclear weapons, I am fairly certain that everybody in the hood gets the point. If we imagine that the much-ballyhooed "Joe six-pack voter" can be swayed with this argument, then your focus group is doing crack. Diplomacy is true strength because of the fact that it is much more difficult to achieve and preserve. What's next? Democrats for Halliburton?

Finally, Joe Biden was ready for his close-up. He did well. He almost cried at this last chance for glory. He looked for all the world like Dorothy in Oz, bewildered but determined. I suppose Joe is the Democrats mean old man to balance off against McCain's finely honed skills in that arena. Fine, then, go get'em Joe.

Wait – there's more... you can't have a baton handoff or torch passing without the successor in the play and like magic, Obama made his mercurial appearance just as the throng was about to head for the exits. All crackling with positivity, he praised the Clintons, easily done now that he was on the throne – if he wins. He embraced his running mate and the entire Biden clan. He is now the man and like an impresario of yesteryear, he gave a taste of the headliner but not the main dish.

Tomorrow the Barack and Roll Circus begins in earnest.

(This article was published on the Huffington Post under the title of, "Bill and Hill Get Back On The Porch; Obama and Biden Hawk Up" – August 2008)

Barack Obama Crosses the Great Divide, Both Ways at the Same Time

August 2008

Complex is the first word that came to mind, while witnessing the Obama launch spectacle. In a scene smack out of a Cecil B. DeMille epic movie, our hero extolled the virtues of the Republic while standing on a stage in a Coliseum. In case you were not aware of that, the backdrop was an ersatz Greco-Roman affair, pillars and all. It is true that if one were to attempt to salvage a Republic, it would be in the midst of a nation bent on Empire. Then again, you wouldn't parade around a bunch of military commanders if you were for peace not war, or would you? Behind the mind of Democratic presidential nominee Barack Obama, lays the mystery of a leader who would be all things to all people.

America is a divided country. Recent presidential elections bear witness to that. Not so, said Barack Obama on Thursday night in D'Town. Mr. Obama proclaimed that there are no Democrats and Republicans; there are only Americans of differing circumstances. It was an echo of the red, white and blue speech that catapulted him to the top of the political heap only four short years ago. Now that I have spent a week immersed in his vision, his organization and his iconic promotion of both, I have gained a better understanding of why he believes that and what makes Obama run.

It has been said that Obama will be the first black President. He will be, sort of. He will also be the next white President, sort of. He will be the first President from the generation following the baby boomers, maybe. In fact, by most definitions he is a baby boomer - anyone born between 1946 and 1964. So, he is of my generation and kind of not really part of us in his mind, as you discover by perusing his marketing plan. What to make of all of this complexity then you may ask? The answer is that within these contradictions lie the rub and the key to our man Obama.

Our motherly apparition of Monday night became poignantly real on Thursday. There she was, with that Mona Lisa smile. Together, all 84,000 0f us, we heard Barack's remembrance of his mother, S. Ann Dunham Soetoro, as pictures from the family album were presented on the jumbo screens above the stadium. It was warm, sad, touching and much more. Ann Dunham crossed the racial divide when she married Barack's father, who was a student from Kenya. Barack Sr. left them after two years and went back to Kenya. Subsequently she married Lolo Soetoro and took Barack with her to Indonesia for five years, where he attended both a Catholic and a Muslim school. Eventually, Barack went to live in Hawaii with his maternal grandparents. Not growing up in a monochrome world, infused our man of the hour with a permanent need to reconcile all sides of every issue to attain balance. It also left him with a lack of decisiveness at critical junctures in governance, when you can't make everyone happy. His non-voting record on a myriad of tough decisions in Illinois and DC are proof of his calculating ways.

We have seen Obama's style of politics before. Bill Clinton was the master of getting ahead by having it both ways. He and his DLC crew presented themselves as "Third Way Progressives." Now there is an oxymoron of particular peckishness. No third way exists in politics. That is exactly what "progressive" politics was designed to combat - standing for nothing and falling for everything. Progressive policy is "Left Turn Only." We will eventually discover if Obama is in fact a disciple of this DLC equivocating.

Standing in Invesco Field, immersed in flags waved in automaton unison, the fireworks evocation of bombs bursting in air, the Protestant remonstrations to secular professions, the chanting of pithy slogans, the generals on parade and the massive pent up desire for hope, change and something to believe in, we were awash in the heady bromide of American incurable romanticism. Americans are especially romantic about the truth concerning themselves. In this obfuscating cloud of emotions, we can easily be manipulated by those who would make us believe we are going forward, only to pick our pockets, while we go nowhere. It is the oldest story in America - the Great Huckster.

I am looking forward to believing in the hope for change. It would be good for all concerned if this is the change it advertises itself as. Realize though, that if we elect Senator Barack Obama and Senator Joe Biden, we will have to do our job. Our prodigious job, as citizens, is to be ever vigilant and demand better from our government. If our government fails us, we must beat it like a rented mule, as they used to say in the Midwest. If it continues to fail to respond then we must replace it, as Jefferson exhorted us to do. As he attempts to cross the great divides among us, Mr. Obama will soon discover that you can't have it both ways at the same time. Leadership is the tough-mindedness to make enemies as well as friends, in the name of the common good, in favor of citizens rather than corporate Cronies. Here's hoping that Mr. Obama gives up the Cheshire cat act and delivers. The proof of the pudding will be in the eating.

(This article, like many of these DNC Convention articles, appeared first in the Valley Democrats United Enewsletter and then in LA Progressive, both its Enewsletter and website, in August 2008)

Meet The Mockers

September 2008

After the din of the desperados of defiant manifest destiny had wafted away across the 1000 lakes of Minnesota. After the air escaped from the red, white and blue balloons. After the moose gutter and the aerial bomber left the building. When all was quiet as midnight rolled across America. Just then, through the obfuscating clouds of impending doom, could we make out the faces of the ever-present jokers of jingoism. Say "hello" voters to our old acquaintances in new faces - meet the mockers.

Oh my - it was all so jocular. One week of solid below the belt punch lines, delivered by the meanest assemblage of carny barkers ever seen outside of a red state fair. There was Giuliani and Thompson, Huckabee and Lieberman, Bush and Bush, on and on, until the lipsticked pit bull bit into the crowd. Yes sir, or mam as it were, she tore into the weak-kneed, dazzling urbanites like a griz comin' out of a hibernation nightmare. Gov. Sarah Palin brought the house down with her sarcasm, wit and relentless mocking atonal attack. It was almost enough to make you forget the issues. Almost.

Then, on Thursday night, the grinning GOP hurdy-gurdy jalopy plopped the prevaricating grand poobah out onto a freshly erected phallic stage extension and Katie bar the door, the Mocker in Chief was in the house. He did it all with a wry smirk but not as coarsely as Fred or Sarah dispatched the heathen enemy, the dreaded Democrat candidate (a pithy mini-mock of particular widespread use among the RNC chatterers), whose name cannot be mentioned. No indeed, Big John McCain, the Mocker in Chief, had come to Minnesota to lay into the big fish - truth, reality, history and the American Way.

Only the fabled Elmer Gantry could have spewed out as many scintillating, spangled and pitch perfect lies, to such a rapturous consumption as McCain let fly, on the last night of the Republican Convention. It was a marvel of Rovian spin skewered on Luntzian misdirection, unequalled in recent memory, other than the sparkling sessions in the last eight years of the White House press briefings.

John pretended that the Democrats had messed everything up in DC and the Republicans were going to go down there and throw the bums out. Change was coming and coming hard. The obvious problem with the pitch was that the Republicans had been in control for the past eight years and were responsible for the mess. To be fair, they were aided and abetted by a gaggle of compliant capitulators from the other side of the aisle. Never the less, sending Republicans to clean out the Republicans was the thrust of the evening; capping a week of pin the tail on the donkey - bizarre but breathtaking in its audacity.

So, dear reader, that's the entire week in St. Paul in a nutshell, except for the copious number of citizens, arrested attempting to exercise their freedom of speech. Both conventions and Parties exhibited a deafening horror at the mere hint of censure. Main Stream Media excised the uncomfortable bits for the fly-over crowd. As the elephant leaves the room, only one more observation remains to be made.

Among the many terms used to define mock or mocking, you will find the following: *to imitate; counterfeit, to treat with ridicule or contempt; deride, simulated; false; sham, in an insincere or pretending manner, to frustrate the hopes of; disappoint.*

It must be assumed that the smart women and men of the GOP/RNC have decided to go with this "mock them to death" game plan for the general election. Given that they have no principled ground to stand on, that makes sense. It is a desperate but clever act. Even though it is a sign of integral weakness, they have used it to great effect before.

Looking out across the roiling swell of querulous everymen and everywomen being jawboned into a frenzy at the Republican Convention, you could plainly see that they were being taken for a ride. By setting up the Democrats as a straw man, alien, fearful and un-American, the vivacious mockers were actually mocking the hopes and dreams of the convocation before them. As John McCain exhorted them to stand up and fight, over and over again, you could hear the change falling out of their pockets, you could see the health vanishing from their families and you knew they were going to vote against their own interests;

easy marks, set up and knocked down by a lustrous old huckster and his leggy side kick - one more massive mockery of America, truth and reality.

I Stand Corrected

November 5th, 2008

Let me be among the first to congratulate my friends, who always believed that Senator Barack Obama would win the election for the Presidency. As most of you know, I was on record one year ago stating that it was my firm belief that America was a country beset by discrimination. Furthermore, that this stain on the character of America's psyche was so strong that neither a woman nor an African-American man could win the coming 2008 election for President. I stand corrected and happily so.

Senator Obama and the millions of Americans who overcame racial prejudice to accomplish this milestone in our history have taken me to school. I have finally been liberated from the shadow of my youth, when the struggles were so vast, civil rights, voting rights, a woman's right to choose, ecological devastation, the Vietnam War and so many other societal ills, that I became trapped in the unending "Culture War". I, like so many others, was pitted against my parent's generation. This developed, over the decades, into the neo-cons versus the Progressives, a bitter and boundless brawl. Eventually, I lost my beginner's mind, where all things seem possible. Thanks to you, Mr. President-Elect, I have regained it.

As I am writing this, Proposition 8 in California, which denies same-sex couples the civil right to marry, appears to have passed. Women will go to work this morning in most occupations and be underpaid compared to their male counterparts. Mentally ill persons, bereft of care and institutions dedicated to improving their lives, will wander the streets of downtown America. In the political arena, America will still have the lowest percentage of women in elected office of any industrialized nation. These and other discriminations remain but today we have hope that they too will be overcome. Today, we can believe again that the future will be better than the past. Today is a very good day, especially for those of us who were wrong about today.

For breakfast, lunch and dinner today, I have prepared for myself generous portions of humble pie. I will happily consume them and toast Barack Hussein Obama - 44th President of the Republic of the United States of America. Today, I will bask in the glow of learning something new. Tomorrow, I will join all of you in the tasks ahead. Be well Mr. President-Elect and thanks for taking me to the woodshed.

Now, about Joe Lieberman...

PART VII

Progressive Economics

Who's "Minding" the Store?
(Or please pass the whole wheat bread)

December 2007

If Calvin Coolidge was right and, *"the chief business of the American people is business,"* then the current management needs to be fired, without a pension. It is bad enough that the Republicans celebrated their unchallenged federal control with wave upon wave of higher and higher deficits but the Democrats giddily joined in, as if their complicity would go unnoticed in the binge of corruption and malfeasance. Moreover, where were all of the Ivy-league MBAs during this collapse of reason? Absent, while searching for their scruples? Is there no decency left? Well, in a word, **no**.

We have quite literally gone to hell in a hand-basket. Perhaps, the current Democratic crew in Congress has the fortitude to stand up to their corporate enablers. Remember though – it is hard to bite the hand that feeds you, so we will wait and see but don't hold your breath dear reader. So, in lieu of any current political leadership - it's time for some new, BIG ideas on how to right the ship of state and clean the Stygian stables of the marketplace.

Herein, I offer the following proposals from a Progressive Liberal Democrat's point of view. They are offered from a sociological as well as an economics perspective, putting people before profit.

Local / Renewable / Sustainable / Humane

If we use those four words – local, renewable, sustainable, and humane – as our maxim, our code of conduct, in the futuring of business, then we can mitigate the disasters that are unavoidable and enhance the possibilities for prevention of the afflictions that are brewing. Narrow self-interests must yield to enlightened self-interests. A little more sharing will go a long way. A cleaner greener world is still possible but time is perilously short.

We must rise to the occasion, open our minds and work together to untether ourselves from the tainted past. We must demand that our elected officials turn the ship of state away from the rocky shoals of stupefied greed. While we are at it, we had better get the looting of the treasury out of their clammy palms with some true transparency. Post all upcoming expenditure bills on the Internet so we can all weigh in on their efficacy before any votes are taken. Make every economic bill a jobs bill, not a corporate profit bill. Make every trade agreement fair not free. End the obscenity of the so-called War on Drugs. Make the tax system progressive not regressive. The better you do in Business America the more you are responsible for maintaining it. Paying more in taxes because you made more in profits as an individual or company is a privilege not a punishment. You owe it to the company that made it possible for you to earn those greenbacks – Business America.

Our American government is the most successful business enterprise in the history of the world - if you insist on looking at it that way. It is time to stop privatizing or selling it off to the lowest incompetent bidder. It is time for all stakeholders to reinvest in our shared responsibility and opportunity.

Like Robert Johnson sang – *we're down at the crossroads with the hellhound on our trail.* As a Progressive Liberal Democrat, I see a possible clean and green future but it will take a massive correction in course for Business America. Cal Coolidge may have been right about something but not about the business of America. When the only business in America is business - with no principles, no ethics - then the business is finished. Put the people before the profit and we can finally get down to business.

Organic / Green Up

It is a happy coincidence that the color of American money is green. After all - Green represents growth, vitality and the unfolding of new ideas. Green represents recycling and clean energy. Green also represents the organic agriculture industry. Over the next decade, organic food will become the dominant symbol of not only good nutrition but also a sustainable planet. Locally grown will broaden the horizon of possibilities for a reinvigorated market system of fair trade. When the counter-culture bloomed in the last century, grocery store shelves carried only white bread with few exceptions. Hippies and New Agers brought consciousness to the health of the nation with the retail availability of "whole wheat bread." This coincided with the publication of the "Whole Earth Catalog." Then came "Earth Day." Now, what seemed bizarre and dangerous has been revealed to be practical and pragmatic. The soundtrack of the "Summer of Love" - do good for all and not just for the few - is becoming mainstream fair trade economics and none too soon.

However, beware dear consumer of the phenomena of "Greenwashing." That is when corporations try to put a positive spin on their products and services by claiming to employ environmentally sound business practices, when the truth is that they are merely painting themselves green and not organically growing themselves green. Take dairy products for instance. If you keep all of your cows in a crowded feedlot and just give them grains and water, you could claim to have "organic" dairy products but that's a stretch. Taste some milk or cheese from cows that roam green fields eating green grass and you will know what I am talking about. Every business has the potential for green, organic growth and sustainability but consumers must remain vigilant as to the truth of every companies "green" bona fides.

Energy Independence

Big Oil is dead. Of course, the big oil operators, private and public have known that for years. They are all for conversion just as soon as they squeeze that last dollar/euro/yen/yuan out of the last barrel of crude. We cannot afford to wait for that outcome. The Republic of the United States of

America should declare a complete end to the use of all energy extractables (oil, coal, natural gas and uranium) in ten years. We should follow the lead of the Apollo Alliance and be bold, like JFK's prediction of putting us on the moon in ten years. There is no need to wait until the science makes this practical. Lead with a BIG idea and the science will follow.

Renewable energy produced here in America along with alternative fuels (wind, solar and geothermal) and conservation is the future. One has to wonder why there is not a LEED "Green Roof" with solar power cells on every public building – city, county, state and federal – in America already. There is a direct line connecting whole wheat bread and the "Prius." Democratic Party leaders should muster the courage to not only discern but also promote it instead of leaving it to the Japanese or Brazilians to show us the way forward.

Healthcare for All

The saying, "an ounce of prevention is worth a pound of cure," was coined by old Ben Franklin. It has never been more apt. With corporations crowding the exits from their responsibilities to their work force past and present, because of the rising cost of private healthcare, it would seem that the time for prevention is at hand. That prevention will be found in Single-payer Universal Healthcare for all Americans. In addition, if that healthcare is led by more preventative medicine, then the costs of cures and procedures will decrease dramatically. America will at last join the civilized world, when the citizens who vote politicians into office will be afforded the same level of healthcare that the politicians vote into law for themselves. All businesses will enjoy more green – profit - with the cost of healthcare off their books. All citizens will enjoy more green – vitality - when their investment – taxes - is vested in their health and well-being.

Drugs & Medicine

All drugs and medicines and their abuse should be reclassified as a medical problem and not a criminal obsession. The legacy of J. Edgar Hoover and the sociopathic leaders of the Twentieth Century must be brought to an orderly close. The War on Drugs is and has always been a war against logic and reason. The Harrison Narcotics Act of 1914 must be repealed. Sadly, only Republican leaders like William F. Buckley, Milton Freidman and George Schultz have had the courage to recognize this glaring reality.

As of yet, there are no leading Democrats, save in the grassroots or at the local level, with the courage to face this calamitous obscenity. Illegal drugs and their cultivation and distribution have undermined every society on the globe so much so that now even once legal over the counter medicines like cold remedies are part of the worldwide trafficking of substances, threatening to bring down civilization as we sit idly by and watch. If you are for the "War on Drugs," then you are for terrorists, gangsters, murder, rape, over-crowded prisons and corruption on a scale not witnessed since the Dark Ages. If it is not the root of modern evil then it is at least the grease on the wheels. The "War on Drugs" is the wellspring of funding for every modern madness - especially organized terror.

Some Democratic leader must summon the mighty courage, as well as loss of vanity and ambition, to lead us out of this purgatory and into a new age of reason. Drugs are a medical problem not a criminal problem.

If we are honest with ourselves and our descendents, we will dry up the swamp of so many of these tyrannies by ending the criminalization of drugs and beginning the era of education, rehabilitation, taxation and legalization.

Investment / Taxes / Infrastructure

Who built the highways that connect every corner of America? Who pays for the police, the fire fighters and the emergency services? Where does the money come from to provide for the common defense? How do we afford municipal water and sewer systems? I could go on but you get the point; we all want these benefits to society and more and somehow they must be invested in for everyone's mutual benefit. We are woefully behind in that endeavor. Katrina's swath of pain is a symptom of the greater cause of this dilemma, which is the failure to secure the infrastructure and invest taxes for the public good.

Our American infrastructure is paid for by our American investment in our government. This is most commonly known as taxes. If you regard America as one large business enterprise, as many conservatives are fond of believing, then we are the shareholders. We are the investors in this enterprise. As stated before, the current management, who work for us, must go. Then we, the shareholders and investors, must reassess where we want our investment dollars, i.e. taxes, to be spent. Unfortunately, Katrina and the crumbling bridges, schools and hospitals of America are currently neglected not only for reasons of corruption and malfeasance but by the so-called Reagan revolution against taxes. Grover Norquist and the sniveling purveyors of, "no more government" – "no more taxes" were bald-faced liars on the hustle for our money and they have gotten way too much of it.

Taxes are not a punishment - unless you are one of the deceitful grifters of the Conservative No-Think tanks - they are an investment. Like most investors we have been happy to let our brokers (politicians) run the investment funds and manage the company until now we find our accounts in the red and we are busted, dead flat broke and headed for monumental bankruptcy. The sub-prime meltdown of 2007 is only the beginning of the Main Street "Global Warming." Be advised though that the pigs at the trough - corporate oinkers and the bleating swine of the political hackocracy - are living high off the investment (taxes) they have stolen from us, the shareholders. There are far too many examples to cite here so just pick one of your local thieves.

Whenever the new Democratic led Congress investigates the waste and fraud, they will not have to look very far to find the missing money in the budget or the waste and the corruption. Just look in the mirror. If you think, I am being unfair, check out how much money each one of them has in their campaign funds treasure chest. A good start to cleaning house would be to call for Full Public Campaign Financing at every level of the government. In fact, that may be the best remedy for everything that ails U.S. It is past time to get a refund on our investment, fire the current managers and get back to building our business – the infrastructure that works for all of us.

Jobs – the Primacy of the Middle Class

Name the most valuable resource in America? In the world? If your answer was – people – then you are a winner! Now, what is the one thing all of the people need to sustain them? A job. Mahatma Gandhi pointed out long ago that the machine was replacing the human hands in the workplace to the detriment of the stability of the community. This lesson was lost on the industrialists, who could only see their own profit – community be damned. That state of affairs was tenable for a period of time but that period has passed.

Even before we run out of the most valuable resources that nature has gifted to us – water, air and land – life will become unsustainable for humans because the parasite will have eaten the host. That is – the ultra-rich and monopolist corporations, which they control, will have devoured so much of the productivity of the working class that the entire scheme of capitalism will fail. With no jobs and no productivity, the working 99% will no longer be able to support the idle 1%. Rome repeats itself on a worldwide scale. Of course this is all avoidable. Good jobs that pay a living wage with benefits and the opportunity to become an owner not just a worker are necessary for a sustainable economy. Somebody tell Wall Street.

Federal fiscal policy, beginning just before 1913, when the 16th amendment to the Constitution was ratified, creating a federal Income tax, has been for more than 100 years chiefly designed to enhance the economic well being of Americans. At least that was the theory. Regrettably though, rich citizens ate the largest part of the pie baked in Congress. Clever prescriptions, like the tragicomically named "minimum" wage, provided flimsy band-aids to the sustained imbalance between rich and poor. Only during the FDR years and into the 60's was public policy generating a more robust middle class. Since the Nixon years, wages have stagnated. This is not only a glaring reason for a true "living" wage but public policy designed to enhance responsible consumer spending. Asking the profligate electeds to lead in responsibility is laughable at best.

A balance between the income of the rich or managers of Business America and the stockholders - workers and citizens of Business America - is necessary to keep the business model sound and afloat. However, the gap between the ultra-rich and the poor is widening at an exponential rate. With more of the wealth created in any society – and wealth is created by the working class not the monied class (e.g. productivity) – going to fewer people at the top, our America as a business model is fatally flawed. Imagine running your own small business, corporation or household where the majority of the profit only went to the top managers. You guessed it – your operations would fail. Who wants to work for nothing? Certainly not the CEOs of corporate America. Warning – kill the buying capacity of the American consumers and the corporations will die. Oh – and do not count on global markets to bail out the craven dismantling of the American working class. Without the American middle class – the global pipedream vanishes. Therefore, it is either more good jobs or too much of nothing. As Bob Dylan wrote, *"too much of nothing makes a man feel ill at ease."*

Public Education

How can you get people to work in the 21st Century jobs when 15 to 20% of Americans are illiterate and only 25% have gone to college? The answer of course is a more robust "Public" education system. However, current educational trends show a stampeding, to the mantra of "privatization," towards charter schools. When this idea – vouchers part II – first crept out of Knoxville, Tennessee, Chris Whittle said that business could educate our children better than the government. In reality, it was just a clever bait and switch game calculated to take the curriculum out of the teacher's hands and the money out of our pockets.

Charter or voucher schools follow a cut and gut philosophy used by take-over specialists to buy then flip undervalued companies. Once they have the green light in any school district, in come their quasi-private schools in place of our public schools. Memorization and testing replace learning and experiential immersion. The arts and physical education are minimized or eliminated. The books are brought in from publishers who toe the new line on just the facts but not the reality in all subjects. Graduation rates are insured at the cost of any semblance of a real or classic education.

Here again, the business model of top-down command creates citizens with a shell of an education. Meanwhile, the public schools are drained of their funds so the test results can show that the charter/voucher schools are better and the downward spiral continues.

It is time to stop this ineffectual shell game and get back to public schools with a broad liberal arts education. A welcome addition would be to offer technical schools as well for those students inclined toward the new technological frontier of the Internet. Every neighborhood should have the best in facilities, books and teachers. To make that possible, teachers should be among the best paid jobs not the least. You can throw in firefighters and police for that raise while you are at it.

Re-Train America

Ok – we get it now. You cannot continue to put an unending stream of automobiles on the face of the planet without disastrous results in air and land use quality. So, let's go back a step to go two forward. We should "re-train" America. Rail travel in all of its forms – light, metro, high speed – is cleaner and greener. As a massive infrastructure undertaking, at all levels of government, it would create more good jobs and new industrial innovations than any other project including space exploration. America's non-productive and pointless war economies could be recycled into heavy industry with a purpose. The world would follow suit if they wanted to keep up. Therefore, more rail travel would lead to less auto travel, creating numerous environmental benefits. Mass transit would at last replace the bloated highway budgets and urban development might be able to come into a sane perspective as well.

Internet / Entrepreneurship

Technology always pushes the past and its masters out of the way. As most business bon vivants are fond of saying – it is amoral. What is immoral is when the power to control technology lays in the hands of an elitist few. Most interesting about the underlying principles of the latest tech tool – the Internet – is that control (favored by the wealthy past) is the antithesis of its fundamental architecture, which is, "facilitation."

Notwithstanding the forgoing statement, major business leaders and old-line businesses are scurrying about trying to devise newer and cleverer ways to subvert the public good and get a grasp on the Internet. Of course, this is futile. For starters, the Internet itself is designed to be so democratic that all tyrannical master plans are merely foolish flops on arrival. More importantly, if allowed to flourish as a democratic technology, former titans of industry stand a better chance at reaping larger profits. Now, that is truly ironic. Again – facilitation of greater participation in the rewards of productivity will increase the bottom line of every interest as long as they are shared interests, e.g. the common good. This is not a new idea limited to technology though. Our Constitution was designed with the same principle in mind – facilitation of the many, rather than control by the few. Hmm – maybe the Founders were on to something!

If allowed to stand as a public utility, maintained for the many not the few, the Internet will provide the greatest advances in entrepreneurship, public discourse and futuring of the Liberal Ideal heretofore known – in America and across the globe. Within the architecture of the Internet, lies the potential for not only the democratization of information but also the democratization of wealth.

Environment / Resources / Recycling

If you need to be convinced that the Climate Crisis is real, then like the dinosaurs you are headed for extinction. If I may presume to speak for the majority of sentient beings though, we don't relish the thought of going down with you. So, what is to be done? How can we save the planet?

Well, the planet doesn't need to be saved. As has been said before, the planet will do just fine if we manage to finish off our miserable existence upon it. It is we, the people, who are in danger of perishing not our mother earth. We can avoid this calamity only if we wake up to the central theme of this entire essay: enlightened self-interest must prevail over narrow self-interest. We are all self-interested. That is a function of our survival instinct. In this decade, millions of years of human evolution have come to the tipping point. Either we all survive and thrive – together – or we all disappear into the echoes of time.

Every being is dependent upon the vitality of every other being. We are inextricably mixed. All resources – especially water – are rare and must be managed for the benefit of each of us. This does not mean that a utopian dream is achievable but without greater sharing and less disparity between the haves and the "ain't ever gonna haves", we are doomed and sooner than we think. Of course, nothing is written yet. Wise use of our most miraculous resource, human reasoning, might just save the day. I think mother earth would like to keep us around for a little longer. Stay tuned.

Last but not least, I think that it should go without saying or contradiction that "recycling" every possible resource is paramount to our design of a cleaner - greener world. We should all start by recycling our outdated notions of I got mine – you get yours.

China Collapses

Amid the furious dash to be embraced by the illusion of billions of consumers eagerly awaiting our every possible trinket, a dark and ominous truth is emerging. Its ramifications promise to annihilate the largest number of humans ever, in one long agonizing fell swoop. I refer to the imminent collapse of Communist China – aided and abetted by globalization and mountainous greed.

Simply put, the industrialized nations' perversion of sound labor practices, as witnessed in the unconscionable abandonment of manufacture in the developed world and the switch to basically slave labor in China, will reap what it has sown. This curse of chasing lower and lower labor costs will come home to roost in horrifying ways that were avoidable and predicted. A century of labor organizing, workplace safety and necessary business regulation will be for naught - especially to the hapless Chinese workers.

Recent discoveries of tainted food and products from China are only the tip of the iceberg of the coming internal Chinese collapse. Imagine what America would be like today if robber baron corporate interests had prevailed here over the last one hundred years. What would life in America be like without laws to protect workers, public safety, food supplies, regulate unsafe manufacturing, reduce pollution, root out corruption and graft, prosecute elected officials who steal from the public treasury, etc.? Yes, I know that many of these protections and laws are not working, as they should here but what if there were none at all? What would America look like then? It would most closely resemble the plot of one of HBO's recent dramatic series. It would start as the Sopranos, evolve into Deadwood and end up as Rome. That is where China exists today. A lawless land pillaged by foreign investment and so-called Socialist or Communist leaders who are nothing more than gangsters. If you're looking for a persuasive argument about the absolute necessity for Labor Unions and the right to organize, not to mention the right to vote, this is it.

Consider just this one scenario of the soon to be Chinese collapse: a healthcare system unprepared for hundreds of millions of emphysema and asthma victims, all showing up at the same time. Besides the monstrous effects of no pollution controls in their air, water or land use, the Chinese have been happily consuming the world's largest number of cigarettes per capita for decades. When the business practices ennobled by Wal-Mart and a host of other companies are combined with the environmental catastrophe fast approaching the Chinese healthcare system, as lacking as it is, will be brought to its knees. Then, the business interests will be unsustainable and the government will disintegrate as the wealthy try to catch the last plane out, stranding the vast majority of citizens.

Running away from everything that made America and its middle class work is going to cost us all dearly – especially the Chinese. As I said, if the business of America is business, then the current management needs to go if only for creating this onrushing gruesome calamity in China.

In Conclusion

There is nothing new in these proposals. These concepts are a compendium of common sense, win-win ideas that were available long before the Hippies and New Agers dared to utter them. Maybe it is their simplicity - as expressed in John Nash's brilliant equilibrium theory - that has made them illusive. Perhaps, it's the venality of the ruling class and their desperate zero-sum proclivity. Of course, there is the inertia of the voting class and their fearful manipulation by political strategists - breeding a catatonic state of disinterest. Whatever the cause, most likely all of the above, the results are killing us.

Progress demands a new idea of community doing business in a local, renewable, sustainable, humane paradigm. All other models have failed and will continue to do so. As a Progressive Liberal Democrat, I believe in a new course of human interaction and interdependency. I have presented a few of the ideas that would make that new world possible. My hope is that collecting these progressive proposals for furthering business into one article will stimulate debate and most importantly – ACTION! Hesitation and obstruction are no longer viable.

Now is the time for change. This is the place for a breakthrough. We are the people who can make it happen. So, please pass the whole wheat bread and let us get back to "minding" the store.

(Many thanks to my editor – Margie Murray – VP Valley Democrats United)

E Pluribus Unum

The Subprime Sucker Punch

February 2008

So, what to do with all of these homes going into foreclosure? Let them go. That's right – walk away from the house. Wait a minute – you are thinking. Are you suggesting that all of these Americans just drop their mortgages and give up on the American dream? No – I'm not. They should realize, that by staying in their dream, they would only wake up to discover that it is a nightmare. The price they bought their home at will not be realized again, unless they stay put for maybe up to ten years. Most of these homes were sold to Americans who couldn't afford them and most importantly at prices that were inflated 100% above what they should have been selling at. These Americans were suckers in a scheme with many deceivers but the sucker punch that will hurt the most is if they stay and continue to pay for all of that equity, which does not exist.

Just as in the 1990's speculative real estate bubble, prices on real estate in the last ten years were gamed by the sellers, flippers and every financial player and institution to create more and more wealth on paper. Rather than continue with sustainable 1 to 2% growth in home values, the rise in prices reached breathtaking double-digit heights in the past two years to as much as 28% year over year in some regions. That type of appreciation is of course unsustainable. Certainly, every player in this giant greater fool scheme knew that - didn't he or she? Well no, they did not.

The greater fool was, as it usually is, the buyer, especially the low-income buyer. Thanks to predatory lending practices, which prey upon low-income, elderly and minority buyers, the lenders were able to create an entirely new group of buyers to fuel their scheme. Some of these buyers may have sensed that buying homes worth hundreds of thousands of dollars with no money down, bad credit and ballooning payments looming on the horizon was a mirage but their need to have a part of the American dream of home ownership was too great. Probably, the largest numbers of these buyers were recklessly unaware of the dangers inherent in their purchase.

So, here comes the Congress to save our hapless fellow citizens. They will do whatever is necessary to keep these good folks in their homes. But wait – this is the bubble inside the bubble - if you stay in your home for let us say, the $300,000 price at which you purchased it. Meanwhile, all of the homes around you are revalued down 30% or perhaps as much as 50%. Then, you are left holding the bag for equity that no longer exists. Equity it will take years and years to just get even with. Why would our saviors from the DC Swamp punish the distressed even further? Because dear reader – the myriad lenders and holders of the bad faith paper, that the home mortgages were rolled into, would be able to save their sagging fortunes on the backs of the suckers. The big guys bottom line would stabilize, while ours would disappear into limitless debt. Now, that's a true roundhouse sucker punch.

Inevitably, the proud and bellicose defenders of free markets, lassiez faire capitalism and neoliberal economic policy, bristle at the thought of government intervention in business, unless and until it comes time to save them from their failures. Then, you and I get to bail them out – think: the Savings and Loan debacle. Yes, smaller non-interfering government is the way to go, trumpet the strumpets of Wall Street but if necessary the public must and will pay the price. That time to save those who refuse to help us with government programs that could help these very same citizens get a real home at a realistic price is here again. At least that's what we are being told.

I favor another approach to this meltdown. Let the people who created the scheme pay for it. Any and every financial institution and lender who participated in the bubble should be left holding the bag, along with the buyers, even the ones who were suckered into it. If the Congress wanted to help, really truly help, the buyers, they should enact a program that let's the buyers default without any harm to their credit rating. Housing prices should be allowed to revalue - decline – and the so-called market should be allowed to fail. If no one pays a price for this deregulated and over speculated financial mess then people will try it again and soon. Buyers who walk away with their credit unharmed will be more financially solvent when the market bottoms out and the home they buy at that point will have a realistic price tag.

Let the free market triumphalists swallow a big dose of the nasty medicine they love to talk about but rarely consume. Let the market and it's failure work. Let the American citizens live to dream another day without paying the bill for the sucker-punch crowd.

PROGRESSIVE ECONOMIC PRINCIPLES:
Creating a Quality Economy

By Mark Pash, CFP
With Brad Parker

May 2008

The economic philosophy of the Progressive Democratic Party is designed to advance human commerce for the betterment of all, while protecting the business environment from itself and the government. Commerce is not perfect and is vulnerable to both human nature and the major flaws of capitalism. The government has to counter the flaws of capitalism, without hindering the market place, and provide a level playing field to insure competition as it facilitates the favorable elements of growth. Economies need checks and balances for successful operations just like the government. Progressive economic principles are the best way to achieve this balance between dynamic fair markets and community interests. Progressive Economic Understanding is the pathway to future financial success for all. "We are all in this together."

In order to better understand the potential of Progressive Economic Principles, we first need to examine the three fundamental flaws of Capitalism. They include:

- **Inadequate Recirculation of Money**

- **Failure to Create Quality Customers**

- **Lack of Long-Term Planning**

THE THREE FLAWS OF CAPITALISM

THE FIRST FLAW:
Inadequate Recirculation of Money

In a free enterprise environment, there is a continual, natural flow of capital to the powerful; the highly educated and already wealthy by various means, both legal and illegal or by shear luck. This natural concentration of wealth continually reduces both the number of businesses and ample individual consumers, eventually hurting commerce and society. All studies, computer models, research and statistics in the past and present validate this scenario.

Concentrated wealth, promoted by this flaw of capitalism, creates a system of, "The Rich get Richer" for both individuals and businesses. This natural bias to the already wealthy reduces competition and the number of adequate consumers. The antitrust laws were established to counter this monopolistic tendency in business enterprises. The fiscal system of taxing the rich and redistribution back to the many was created to solve this problem on an individual basis.

Adam Smith stated: "capitalists left to their own devices would rather collude than compete." This means the natural goal of a commercial enterprise is to attain monopoly status, control or own all or most of their market. (The healthcare industry, medical insurance and pharmaceutical companies are prime modern day examples) This coincides well with the natural goals of many individuals to become as rich as possible. Both Republicans and Democrats have recognized this flaw. In 1890, the Republican Party passed the Sherman Antitrust Act, which was enforced by Republican President, Theodore "Teddy" Roosevelt. Years later, the Democratic Party started the Keynes fiscal policy of redistribution of income and wealth under Franklin Roosevelt.

This is why it is very important to have an adequate antitrust policy and enforcement. The more competition the better! Competition creates more employment, which creates more customers. It rewards efficiency, with profits and with losses, and makes it more difficult for individuals and businesses to gain monopolistic control of the marketplace. Diffusing power and distributing wealth are essential to creating a healthy business environment. If we cannot have this multi-firm free market competition, then we have to regulate the monopolies and oligopolies, including prices, to stimulate more competition.

Frankly, I think the word "redistribution" is the wrong word to describe this policy. It should be called "recirculation." The vast majority of government spending including military is allocated domestically. It is not hoarded so that its recipients can live on its return. It is recirculated through the economy. These monies collected by taxes are spread to more individuals creating better consumers. These consumers are able to spend more in private enterprises, which create wealth for certain capitalists and to some extent for their employees. Unfortunately, this system can be thwarted to achieve the aims of the few rather than the many.

The resistance to the proven Keynesian fiscal philosophy of redistribution persists in the current conservative industrial and political leadership as they resist most types of government spending except military. By not believing in Progressive Economic Principles, they hinder the creation and improvement of effective recirculation programs. They may be politically expedient in supporting certain types of these spending programs, of which Social Security and Medicare are the largest, but by not believing in and in fact hindering effective recirculation, they put capitalistic societies in danger from economic depression-recession or outright revolution.

THE SECOND FLAW:
Failure to Create Quality Customers

In most competitive business environments, there is a conflict between managing for a profitable business and paying adequate wages to create a quality consumer. Owners want to pay employees as low as possible to increase their profits. This results in the creation of inadequate customers. To compensate for this effect, the government's domestic spending agenda helps under-paid workers by providing such programs as education, medical, and retirement benefits etc. that they cannot afford to purchase. Perversely, it is usually these same conservative business owners who oppose these benefits! Labor unions, labor laws, minimum wages and labor regulations offer assistance in overcoming this major problem in our world today. However, quality customers can only be created by paying wages high enough to sustain and enhance every worker's ability to purchase quality goods and services. **Therefore, we should develop standards for a quality customer minimum wage instead of the present understanding and application of just a minimum wage.**

There is no such thing as a competitive labor market, not with billions of people in poverty and low cost slave labor. These people do not make good customers. This is a major global problem. The challenge is running a business - microeconomics - with a customer base drawn from a fully employed and adequately compensated work force. There should not be any significant competition within any industry based on hourly wages, for the same job within a geographical region. Competition should be based on many other business factors including labor utilization. Competition for labor, based solely on low wages, reduces the number of customers and their ability to buy more goods and services.

There is a myth that wages should be left to the free market mechanism. This natural inclination of a business owner-manager is to either minimize his labor force or pay less for labor so he can make more profit. Corporate downsizing and offshore flight to cheap labor markets provides classic examples of this decision-making. Granted, these are correct business decisions for increasing profit. But, if all businesses in the economy implemented these policies, their sales will retreat drastically because their customers would not be well paid enough to buy their goods and services. This was basically the cause of the great depression in the 1930's and the many other severe economic conditions that preceded it.

The world's production systems can produce enough for everyone - supply - but the demand is not there because the people do not make enough to buy it. When mass production is accompanied by mass consumption, a more evenly spread distribution of wealth occurs. Since wealth is tied to both production and consumption, the economy thrives.

Therefore, businesses should not compete based on the payroll cost of individual workers. They should compete on the many other factors of business such as, labor utilization, marketing, operational efficiencies, management, innovation and quality. Henry Ford was the first to get this right, by almost doubling the daily wages of his workers, so they could buy his Model-T. The economists and businessmen of the day thought this was going to be an economic disaster. They were obviously wrong.

The argument is that the price of goods will substantially increase if wages are raised. The labor cost component is not the only component in the pricing mechanism. A reasonable increase in wages (fringe benefits) does not increase prices at the same rate. It is usually much smaller. Also, wages are deductible so any increases are partially paid by reduced taxation. Therefore, prices can go up somewhat but customer demand goes up also, creating more employment as well as a better economic and community environment. There are rising wages in the current capitalistic system but not enough to create an adequate diverse consumer base.

What currently hides this flaw – creating the quality customer - is consumer debt - credit cards, equity lines of credit and the necessity for working spouses. The government has helped to abate this problem with substantial government employment. The great depression was caused when the public had no access to credit when the Fed tightened monetary policy because their wages could not sustain the economy.

As capitalism gets more efficient it generally requires less labor to produce all the needed goods and services. Of course, this means less customer purchasing power - demand. Thus far, capitalism in the United States has solved some of this problem through innovation and the creation of new goods and services, some of which did not exist a few years ago. But, successful capitalism still might mean a larger government involvement both on a fiscal and monetary basis. **In the end, creating quality customers through higher wages is paramount to keeping up demand for goods and services and completes the recirculation cycle.**

THE THIRD FLAW:
Lack of Long-Term Planning

There is the obsession with immediate - short-term - maximization of profits - "The Quick Buck." Private capital and management are constantly expecting relatively quick and high rates of return. Government capital is more long-term and not profit oriented, so it works more for the benefit of society, including business. We see this clearly in the investments in infrastructure, education, research and other necessary projects. Government regulations and tax policies should always encourage more long range planning in the private sector.

An excellent example of encouraging long-term planning in the private sector is tax policy on dividends. They should be taxed at the same rate to individuals as wages are, with a small exclusion for lower income earners. However, they should be deductible to the corporations, the same as interest on their debt. This would encourage more equity capital and dividend payouts instead of accumulation. Thus, having the tremendous effect of trying to maintain the dividend resulting in better long-range policies than short-term profits for current stock trading. **Generally a business will make substantially more money over time because it survives longer with appropriate long range plans and operations.**

Pollution is another notable example. Does it pay to maximize short-term profits by disregarding appropriate pollution controls resulting in costly clean ups, fines and possible extinction, not to mention killing your customers or making them sick so they have to spend more on healthcare instead of your companies goods and services? No, it does not. Pollution controls greatly enhance the long-term benefits not only to humans but also to all businesses - especially the sectors they regulate.

Remember - the total of long-term profits will always be greater than the sum of all short-term profits added together! Long-term planning yielding long-term profits for both business and the community are the most sustainable economic model over time.

Summary of the Three Flaws of Capitalism

Government funded programs, such as education, unemployment compensation, wage-protecting tariffs and laws, and minimum wages are a necessity. In the general global economic debates, especially after the fall of communism and the unsuccessful socialistic efforts, we hear very little of the flaws of capitalism - free market systems. But, like all human endeavors, these flaws definitely exist and it is important for public and private institutions alike to help overcome them if we want to expand our economic future on this planet.

Capitalism does significantly raise the standard of living but not for all and not enough for many. Therefore, it is up to government to take a more active role in the economy in order to overcome these flaws with as little hindrance as possible. In other words, one of the major missions of a federal government has to be macroeconomic well being. But, the vigorous policies of government can also promote private solutions to these flaws. Private philanthropic and labor union measures can be encouraged, as can pension programs, profit sharing and equity sharing plans, job training, child care and medical insurance.

For some reason, many do not believe that these flaws exist. All they have to do is look at the economic record prior to the extensive gov't involvement starting in the mid 1930s: the panics of 1837, 1857, 1873, 1893 and 1907; the Banking Crisis of 1884; the recessions of 1892-6 and 1921; the severe depression from 1873 to 1879 and the Great Depression of the 1930s. The record after this period of the modern industrial age is much less volatile with the average population living substantially better lives because steps were taken by the government to correct the flaws of capitalism.

Although we will be discussing these flaws, and other areas of how to improve our capitalistic system, it might seem to be an overly negative analysis of capitalism. Therefore, I want to impress on you the enormous success of our system, which provides the tax dollars and wealth to fund our government. There is a necessity not to hinder capitalism but to enhance it thru effective government policies.

ENHANCING FREE MARKETS - CAPITALISM

Enhancing the system of capitalism increases the total tax revenue, which helps the government provide the services that are needed. The government should pursue policies that encourage and facilitate business formations, operations and competition. Local and National governments need to reduce or maintain low the barriers to the formation of new businesses - entrepreneurship. The government can also play a key role in entrepreneurship by improving the environment for entry and operations. All government fiscal policies need to encourage and not hinder incentives, initiative, innovation, productivity, investment, research and development. The government always needs to continually simplify tax laws and regulations - red tape to facilitate business growth. It needs to not over-regulate the good but look more for the bad and increase their punishments. Government needs to insure a level playing field in the business environment to insure fair competition.

The government must discourage competition within an industry and geographical area based on the cost of an individual's labor, as that reduces the quality of customers. It needs to insure labor utilization and flexibility of hiring and firing while protecting employee rights and unemployment benefits. It needs to create portability of benefits, income tax averaging and other features for today's more mobile labor force. Government fiscal policy can boost productivity by creating more accessible and affordable quality education for all thus creating a more capable labor force.

GLOBALIZATION & TRADE

Globalization is the continual increase and expansion of commerce by individual firms worldwide. As a consequence, this is producing the gradual elimination of national boundaries, where commerce is concerned. However, these firms are basically in competition with each other not with individual countries. Eliminating boundaries has generated both positive and negative effects. The three flaws of capitalism have followed globalization and must be dealt with on an international level.

There are limited international regulatory bodies to oversee these firms except the World Trade Organization, which does not have much power. Obviously, we will need to develop more institutions for this purpose. It will be a major task for future administrations to comprehensively address these issues. So, how can we compete as a nation when our firms and other country's firms buy, sell and produce all over the world to take advantage of these flaws of capitalism? We cannot! **Therefore, the major area of concern for our government is and should be the economic well being of our people, our customers. The concept of a well-compensated work force, thus creating quality customers, is the major objective of every nation. In order to rebalance global trade and wages, we must have the wages of the international work force progress towards us and not ours being lowered to theirs.**

Countries like China are attempting to compete as a country not as independent businesses. The government owns many, if not all of their companies. This is a socialist scheme not capitalism. They compete by making use of flaw number two, outlined above. They are taking advantage of the huge consumer base (middle class) in the United States. The major long run problem with this strategy is that it is not building a large enough adequate consumer base in China. If the U.S. consumers slightly lower their consumption because of lower wages, less credit card and home equity-line debt or a basic recession, China could see a significant recession/depression.

Since the U.S. is still the primary customer, it has the power to use tariff changes, not to protect industries but to protect the middle class purchasing power and more importantly - to force low wage countries to pay an adequate wage so they can become adequate consumers. **We do not have to insist on equal wages but reasonable non-slave labor wages that are rising to continue to allow access into our markets. Yes, Labor Unions are an additional method to help accomplish an adequate consumer base goal but tariff changes are needed as well.** The concept of Americans having super cheap goods and services, which offsets our wage declines, is absurd. This differential, so we can buy 10 shirts instead of 9, is not economically justified when those workers, who make the shirts, can't buy any of our production of goods and services. Furthermore, the increase in the labor component of manufacturing in other countries will not significantly raise prices to alter our consumer habits. We should eliminate or reduce all tariffs on countries with adequate wages and environmental practices. We should raise tariffs on all those who do not. Also, we should probably continue with a small general tariff on all goods as a revenue raising structure in addition to taxes.

The excessive trade deficit is deceiving to some degree as well. It does not include monies coming into the United States in terms of education of foreign students, investments in stocks, real estate and government bonds. They receive our paper and we receive their goods and services. What it does mean is that foreign individuals, enterprises and countries will own our assets as we will own theirs. This is true globalization! How do we compete in this environment? The solution is to reduce our dependence on foreign oil and create an increase in the wages of other countries, through tariff increases, so their workers can afford to buy our goods and services.

The "Fair Trade vs. Free Trade" argument is somewhat bogus as almost all industrialized countries have some sort of tariffs. I am for total free trade with the proper tariffs to protect the consumer base-wage differentials, ecological differences and anticompetitive practices (dumping & subsidies) by governments with large pocket books. **Our firms can compete with any firm globally - they only need a relatively level playing field.**

TAXES

There are many websites, newsletters, books, etc. on tax policy. Following are only the general important concepts and the defense of Progressive tax policy.

The Progressive Income Tax is one of the fairest taxes as it is based solely on the ability to pay. What is important is not how much any individual earns but how much is left over to be an adequate consumer and saver for retirement. This bears repeating: It is not important how much one pays in taxes but how much money is left after paying taxes! Creating quality consumers is essential to tax policy and therefore the Progressive Income Tax is the key to sound government fiscal policy in offsetting flaw number one.

The estate tax is also a very fair tax because the taxpayer is dead and no longer in need of their money. It is levied only on the very, very rich. It is the best tax to offset the first flaw above - the rich getting richer - which reduces the number of consumers and the ability to build wealth. Importantly, there are provisions to help family farms and businesses. And, contrary to some opinions, many of these assets have never been taxed!

Collectibility in tax legislation always has to be considered in specific tax regulations and laws. The capital gains rate at 15% is substantially below the maximum wage rate at 35%. But, the lower the capital gains rate, usually, the more transactions resulting in more total tax revenues. Ease of tax avoidance and evasion is also a consideration.

Tax Deductions and Credits can also be used to offset business risk and encourage social behavior.

Payroll-FICA-Social Security Tax is an income tax. It needs to be included in any income tax debate as more workers pay a higher payroll tax than income tax. It is not as progressive as the income tax because it is a flat tax with a ceiling. A great tax cut for 95% of the workers and many small businesses in the country would be a reduction in the employee based tax rate and elimination of the ceiling. This could be structured to be revenue neutral or a revenue increase to actuarially extend social security.

Lowering or raising income taxes does not necessarily create a boom or bust. There are many other factors involved. Most of these taxes are usually spent, as the government is the customer - offsetting flaw number two. The Clinton Administration raised taxes in the early 1990s and we had the biggest boom in the history of mankind. The income tax rate in the early 1930s, during the Hoover Administration, was 24% on only the wealthy and we had the worst depression in modern industrial history. Of course, no government taxing system can be too confiscatory resulting in overly restricting and reducing the incentives of the free enterprise system.

In other words, a tax rate of 99% is too high and 1% is far too low to overcome the flaws of capitalism. The Clinton years seems to depict an appropriate level of taxation. Personal and corporate tax rules; regulations and preparation should be kept as simple as possible. This does not mean reducing the number of brackets or itemized deductions but mostly the above the line regulations.

Corporate tax rates should be more progressive as they have more of the ability to pay as it is based on profits after salaries and expenses. It should be lowered for smaller and less profitable businesses and increased on more profitable corporations. Of course, the very significant corporate loophole system and offshore havens always needs to be reviewed and corrected, which will allow actual rates to be lower without losing revenue.

One has to be careful with taxes based on sales not profits; sales taxes, consumption taxes, the VAT tax and property taxes. They can over-interfere with commerce and are usually over burdensome for lower income families and businesses.

Should the tax on dividends be so substantially below the taxes on interest and wages? The answer is - no. Dividends should be taxed at the same rate as everything else with exclusion for a small amount of dividends and interest so it will stimulate and help the lower income families save for retirement. In fact, the dividends paid out by corporations should be tax deductible with offsetting increases in taxes to make it revenue neutral. This will encourage corporations to plan more for the long term, which addresses flaw number three. These increased dividend payments will help the Baby Boomer Bubble through retirement without any requirement to sell securities.

There is an argument that individuals end up paying all taxes either directly or through high prices. This is not a completely accurate statement. Although, this is somewhat true because we are all in the system, it is an unrelated argument because what counts is how much a business or individual has left over after taxes. Also, pricing mechanisms include many costs and other factors of which taxes are only one of them. Taxation comes out at various points of the production-sales-profit cycle. The question is at what point does it come out?

MONETARY POLICY

Monetary Policy (the creation of new money) is as economically important as fiscal policy (how much the government taxes and spends). Currently, the monopoly of creating and distributing new money is accomplished by the commercial banking system - i.e. Bank of America, Wells Fargo etc. - by the creation of debt. We thought it was well controlled and regulated by the Federal Reserve – central bank, until the recent sub-prime fueled financial crisis. We have learned that no matter how much regulation there will always be errors in a human system.

Over the last two hundred years, we have seen many monetary crises in every country on the globe. There are many reasons for these failures, such as over-corrections, mismanagement, cronyism, familism, corruption, and political interference. Since human behavior is not perfect, when this single system over lends, usually in the booming sectors, it has substantial problems when those sectors start their decline. Also, having one system with its strict guidelines reduces competition and diversity. "You can only borrow if you already have money – collateral!" This means the single banking system for the distribution of new money is too limited and too under-diversified in its infusion of new money. This stifles growth, competition, the recirculation of money and employment.

These failures can be drastically reduced in two major ways: (1) by having many systems deliver new money reducing the ravages of human error; (2) and by educating the public with full disclosure and transparency regarding monetary and financial functions and products.

The banking system will remain the major source for the monetary system for some time. I am recommending that the Federal Reserve increase the commercial banking system's reserve requirement by a small percentage. This allows them to distribute some new money through many other new distribution institutions under their control. Some of these new monetary delivery systems should have an equity return not just an interest rate charge - or combination thereof. This reduces the extreme negative effects of high interest rates causing failures - defaults - and the reluctance of private enterprise to invest.

The evolution of our monetary system, which is based on an archaic banking structure, developed several centuries ago, needs modernization. The future evolution of our monetary system is of vital importance. It can

fund appropriate programs that have a return relieving the burden on the fiscal side of government.

EDUCATION

Education is very, very important to individuals in a capitalistic system - especially math and science education in our high tech world. It is also very important to a democratic society in general. But, it is only one of the important components for a successful economy. Brazil, Russia and India - before recent economic booms - had well-educated populations with nominal success economically.

What is important in the United States is that we must begin to educate the general population in matters of personal finance and capitalism. We live in capitalistic society and world. The more educated the public is - the less reliant they will be on government-fiscal programs. Every high school student should be required to take a course in personal financial planning in order to graduate.

Since money can be created at no cost by the government, except for excess inflation, and education is a primary social policy, the government can make long-term college loans - 20 to 30 years - at a cost of about 3%, with repayment starting after graduation. The interest charge just covers administration costs and defaults. The government does not have to make a profit and it does not matter how long it takes to be repaid, as long as it is repaid. This allows almost everyone to afford a student loan and relieves the burden on the fiscal side of government.

STATISTICS AND FORMULAS

Beware of economic Statistics and Formulas. They reduce the human economic conditions to numbers and we over rely on them. They can be unreliable from errors in collection and they can be interpreted in many different ways. Most of the economists do not agree on their own definitions like growth and productivity. The savings statistics are also very misleading. They do not include pension contributions and subtract them when they are paid out. They also do not include investments. The highest savings rate in the world is in Japan, which has been in a deep recession for 15 years.

OWNERSHIP

Ownership should be encouraged for everyone in a capitalistic system. It is very difficult to continue to raise wages so that workers can save and build wealth. Therefore, the government, to promote ownership by every citizen, should implement laws and regulations that enhance that outcome. Not necessarily direct ownership in business and real estate but in stock markets and other equity avenues. We should continue to encourage all pension, profit sharing, ESOP, 401k, and IRA plans. In the long run, it will mean less reliance on government fiscal services.

INFLATION

Moderate inflation is good and excess Inflation is bad. Growth and wage increases do not cause inflation in the overall economy. The economic boom in the 1990s proved this. The only thing that creates excess inflation is too much money issued by the banking system and Federal Reserve chasing an inadequate supply of goods, services and assets.

BALANCED ANNUAL FEDERAL BUDGET

A balanced annual budget has a positive compounding effect. It generally lowers interest rates. This means the interest charges on the total national debt declines. This makes it easier to balance the budget and/or increase fiscal spending. Since there is no new debt added, the national total debt can be retired by the gradual monetarization of the debt by the Federal Reserve without excess inflation. This again makes it easier to balance the budget. So, the comments we often hear, that building debt that our children and grandchildren have to pay off, is not completely true.

Of course, in an extreme recession or war a budget deficit might be warranted. I foresee a possible deficit used for Medicare to get the baby boomer generation through retirement. Therefore, it is important to balance the annual budget as soon as possible.

USURY

In the not too distant past, certain principles of money were not subject to alteration by society's money managers. They might be ignored or forgotten for a time but they could not be repealed. One of these principles was the ancient biblical injunction against usury. The definition of usury may have vacillated over the centuries but the moral meaning was the same. When lenders insisted on terms that were sure to ruin the borrowers, this was wrong. This was usury.

There were practical, as well as moral reasons, why usury was considered a sin. It was more than a social plea for fairness and generosity from the wealthy. No social system could tolerate usury, not as a permanent condition, because it led to an economic life that was self-devouring. The money monger collected his due until he owned all the property and the peasants had nothing. No one could really survive. Who would buy from the money monger if he had all the money? And what kind of life would the peasants have?

We have had usury laws in our country. Currently there are none. Consequently, moneylenders can charge as high a rate of interest as they want - 20%, 30% or more. Usury laws pegging the highest rate that can be charged to the Federal Reserve Funds rate must be enacted to preserve the buying power of the quality customer and reduce bankruptcies. Those rates must be reasonable for both the lender and the borrower.

PROGRESSIVE ECONOMIC PRINCIPLES

- Capitalism is a wonderful freedom-oriented and wealth-building system. It is the best economic system on earth but it is NOT PERFECT.

- Economies need checks and balances for successful operations just like the government.

- Reduce competition based on minimizing wages as it reduces the number of quality customers.

- Insure more long-range planning by business and government - i.e. infrastructure, education, and environment - long-term versus short-term profits.

- Promote competition by limiting and/or regulating monopolies and oligopolies.

- Balance the fiscal budget except for severe recessions and/or war.

- Government spending is not anti-growth it is a recirculation (redistribution) program that aids the economy. It provides for an ample supple of quality customers.

- Government policies need to encourage and not hinder business formations, operations, incentives, initiative, innovation, productivity, investment, competition, research and development.

- Government needs to insure a level playing field in the business environment to insure competition.

- Governments need to insure Property Rights are always protected while also protecting human rights and community interests (i.e. the rule of law).

- Governments should not over regulate the good but look more for the bad and increase their penalties.

- Taxation should not be based on how much one pays but how much one has left over to raise a family - be a quality customer - and save for retirement. Progressive Income and Estate taxation are the fairest taxes as they are based more on the ability to pay.

- We need to compete on a global basis by protecting the wages of our customers and encouraging other countries to do the same. This is accomplished by a change in our current tariff charges and by encouraging the formation of labor unions.

- Insure there is an ample supply and diversity of access to capital from our monetary system with interest and equity return.

- Moderate Inflation is good. Excess Inflation is bad.

- Beware of economic statistics and formulas.

- Encourage ownership and financial education by all.

- The government can fund it but it does not have to run it. Governments can fund, regulate and operate certain functions if they do not lend themselves to market competition.

- The question is not more or less government involvement in the economy but the right government involvement in the economy.

- Implement a variable maximum percentage interest that can be charged on loans, so that we can avoid usury in our credit system.

VISION FOR A PROGRESSIVE ECONOMIC FUTURE

The conflict between business and social interests does not arise from the entire capitalistic system itself but from it's three major flaws:

- **Inadequate Recirculation of Money**

- **Failure to Create Quality Customers**

- **Lack of Long-Term Planning**

In order to create a quality economy we must commit ourselves to overcoming the flaws of capitalism, while steadfastly following the essential Progressive Economic Principles. Conservative Economic Policy has run into a dead end. Progressive Economic Principles can rescue America and the world from this calamity and lead us into a future where wealth is created and enjoyed by every citizen in a quality economy by creating a new framework of economic decision-making. Capitalism and social well being are not antithetical but are both enhanced when the government is run with sound progressive economic policies.

A properly empowered government with an intelligent mandate, both monetary and fiscal, can accomplish these objectives for the 21st century. However, the current structure of a significantly unbalanced budget and an expansive single monetary distribution channel - banking - does not completely meet the needs of the economy and usually causes excess or hyperinflation. Any government policy that combines the opposite, both a constrictive fiscal and monetary policy, can only lead to a disastrous recession or depression.

The current structure does not make common sense for long-term growth. Keep in mind though, that changing a major structure and operational system is very difficult to accomplish, especially in good times let alone bad. Change has to be slow and gradual to reduce economic turbulence.

One of the major structural changes should be to continually increase investment by diversifying the monetary delivery systems. The major problem with capitalism is that governments do not increase the monetary supply in an efficient manner. The best doctrine is an expansive fiscal policy with no deficits and an expansive monetary policy with multiple delivery channels under the central bank - Federal Reserve.

In an economy guided by Progressive economic principles the legislatures will continue to fight over how much to tax, regulate and where to spend. What is eliminated is the economic philosophical debate that the government should not be involved in the economy and the death of laissez-faire-libertarian economics, forever. The legislatures should also debate over the best policies to increase competition and promote growth in our economic environment.

Another major challenge for future governments is; how do we combat the flaws of capitalism in a globalized economy, where enterprises move from country to country to avoid regulation and the flaws? Eventually, in a Century or so, they are going to run out of countries! It is also very important in the debate on reducing the negative effects of globalization to include suggestions on creating a global level playing field and promoting growth in the entire global economy. Remember that increased growth brings in more tax revenues, without increasing rates, for our favored fiscal long-range programs, which advance the human condition. Economic logic is circular. It is not linear. Everything affects everything else.

With this economic blueprint I have endeavored to provide the Democratic Party with an outline that charts a path to the future. My hope is that Democratic and Republican elected officials as well as candidates and economists will study these concepts and implement them at every level of our government.

We can expand the economy by reducing the flaws of capitalism and encouraging the favorable factors of commerce. This increases the standard of living for all, while eliminating poverty. Thus, capitalism becomes a system that provides for all even though many have more. Diversity of ownership further enhances this growing sustainable economic possibility for the entire globe.

Creating long-term wealth for the maximum number of quality consumers is the direct product of creating a quality economy. Creating a quality economy requires a more reasoned knowledge of and application of Progressive Economic

Principles, which create the quality customer and entrepreneurial opportunity for the greatest number of citizens. Economic well being for all requires a balance between business and community needs that work together in everyone's best interests.

We need to explore the solar system, the seas, cure diseases, stop poverty and urban blight, and promote democracy and capitalism in the old Soviet bloc and Third World nations. We are capable of accomplishing most of these tasks. The only thing stopping us is macroeconomics.

Macroeconomic policy based on Progressive Economic principles will offset the flaws of capitalism creating an adequate standard of living and community for all. By raising overall business growth through competition and diversity we will foster local, sustainable, renewable and humane communities living in a quality economy.

CODA

RENEWAL 2009

December 2008

Tis' the season. Yes, beloved community - it is the season again for renewal. Let us all renew our efforts towards a progressive liberal democratic America and world. Let us reaffirm our commitment to each other, to our forgotten ancestors and to the future we will not see but will be a part of.

Take a moment to reflect on the successful election of a new Democratic federal government. Take a moment to thank our lucky stars that once again we have the chance to go further. Take a moment to contemplate the continuing struggle for equality, justice and opportunity we know awaits us in 2009. Then act and act now.

Most of all - as we celebrate our families and reach out to help others, as we raise our voices for truth and tolerance, as we remind ourselves to be inclusive not prohibitive - remember to nourish your sense of humor. We all know the continuing horrors of the modern world are surrounding us but if we seek to bring light to this dark moment then let us do it with a sense of humility and warmth that leads to humor.

I think Molly Ivins, I. F. Stone, Oscar Wilde, Studs Terkel and Mark Twain would all remind us to renew our spirit along with our insight and outrage. If you can't laugh at yourself and the human circus then you won't keep your own hope alive let alone foster it in others.

So, rejoice, renew and remind yourself of all that we have been through and all that we can do together. Keep it real and keep on pushin'.

Here's to a better world and a Happy New Year for all in 2009!

About the Author…

Brad Parker is a prolific political writer and speaker as well an award-winning recording artist, songwriter, producer and musician. Brad has been involved with many Democratic Party organizations including: Officer of the Progressive Caucus of the California Democratic Party, President of Valley Democrats United in the San Fernando Valley of Los Angeles, Board of Trustees of Progressive Democrats of America, Vice President of Progressive Democrats of Los Angeles, Delegate to the California Democratic Party Central Committee from the 42nd and 41st Assembly Districts. Parker has worked with many leading Democrats including Vice President Al Gore and Tom Hayden. He is a contributor on economic issues at the Progressive Economics website - www.economicsfordemocrats.com. Brad has recorded, toured and produced hits in North America, Europe and Asia. Parker owns Indie label Riozen Records and is a co-founder of www.muzlink.com. Brad Parker's website is: www.riozen.com.

further…

Made in the USA
San Bernardino, CA
14 March 2017